Denmark from Above

AERIAL PHOTOGRAPHY
Hans Henrik Tholstrup

AUTHOR
Henning Dehn-Nielsen

FREDENSBORG SLOTSHAVE

LAYOUT
H. C. Steensen

HANS HENRIK THOLSTRUP PUBLIKATIONER A/S

Denmark from Above

Copyright © Hans Henrik tholstrup Publikationer A/S
Ariel Photography by Hans Henrik Tholstrup
Authored by Henning Dehn-Nielsen
Translation by Henrik Holstein
Layout by Hans Christian Steensen

Thanks to
Lui Brandt
Brian Sandberg & Jens H.T. Larsen

Print by Nørhaven Book A/S
1. Edition, 2004
www.hanshenriktholstrup.dk
ISBN 87 989875-1-8

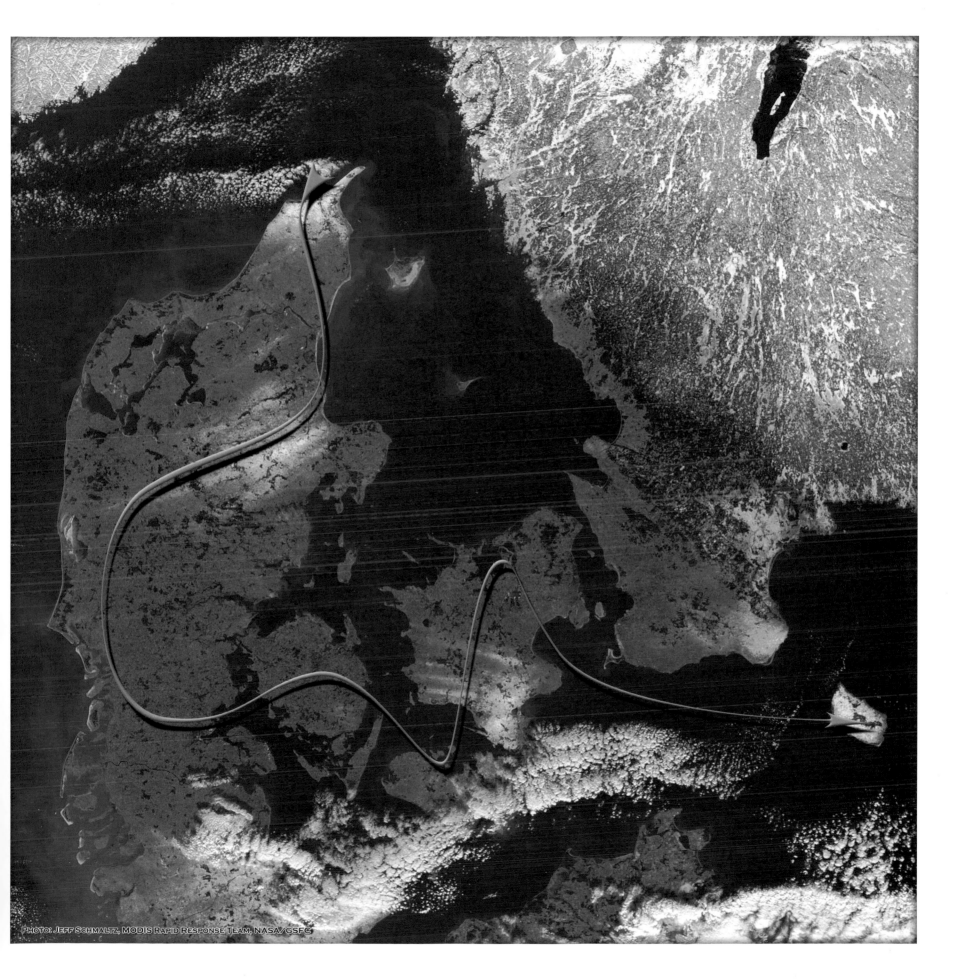

OY-HHT

This Bell Jetranger OY HHT is the helicopter from which the arael photograher and pilot Hans Henrik Tholstrup will let us see his beautiful and prosperous country, Denmark. The trip starts at the northermost point of the country, Skagen, continues down through Jutland, Funen, Zealand and the southern islands to end on the island of Bornholm in the Baltic Sea.

Love does not consist in gazing at
each other, but in looking outward
together in the same direction.

Antoine de Saint-Exupery
(1900-1944)

GRENEN

It is far from certain that the ever active sand spit which represents the extreme point of Jutland between Skagerrak and Kattegat and the peninsula of Skagens Odde will look like this picture next time it is visited. Grenen is a piece of Denmark under constant transformation due to the rolling waves passing by and the enormous amount of water and sand, drifting in here from the west coast of Jutland, carried by a stream parallel to the coast. On a yearly basis about 1 million cubic metres of sand and gravel is moved around to the north-eastern submarine reef of Skagen, while the south-east coast is exposed to a powerful erosion. It is believed that the peninsula has moved more than one km to the north within the past 200 years because of the sedimentation. It is the northern part of the country that is protruding, while materials continiously are being moved from the southern side of Grenen and the reef to the northern beach, the most northern point of Denmark. The entire area with its dunes, moors, wet hollows and stony plain, amounting to a total area of 350 hectares, became a protected area in 1940. This protection was extended to include the area around "Det Hvide Fyr" - the White Lighthouse. Other than this there are attractions such as the reconstructed tilting lighthouse, "Skagens Fyr", the modern lighthouse of Skagen West, the grave of the painter and poet Holger Drachmann, the Grenen Museum of Art, and the attractive Skagen Odde Nature Center, established 1997-2000, designed by the famous Danish architects Jørn and Jan Utzon.

THE SANDCOVERED CHURCH

Besides Grenen, Skagen and Råbjerg Mile, the church buried in sand in the uninhabited and harsh dune area, some 2-3 km southwest of Skagen, is one of the big tourist attractions of the area. Originally the Gothic long-house church, as much as 45 metres long, must have been built shortly after year 1400 and was consecrated to the popular Saint Lawrence. Decades of heavy sand drifting moved sand into the church and blocked its entrance, and in 1775 after especially heavy drifting the nearby farms, houses, and fields were abandoned. 20 years later the church was abandoned, too, and only the tower was left - as a landmark for the sailors. When the nave was torn down in 1810, it is believed that the walls were covered by sand, up to a height of 6 m. The remaining upper part of the tower was declared protected in 1903 and is now maintained by the State. It is assumed that at the eastside of the tower a wall-base up to 3 m high, and several gravestones are hidden and possibly also the limestone font, presumed to originate from Gotland in the Baltic Sea, but so far no major research has been carried out on the remains of the big church. The present church in the town of Skagen was erected in 1841 after drawings by the neo-classicistic architect C.F. Hansen and was reconstructed by the architect Ulrik Plesner in 1909-10.

RÅBJERG MILE

You feel like in Sahara when in the middle of Denmark's only existing, uncontrolled wandering dunes. Råbjerg Mile is a dune formation, 1 km wide, 2 km long, and at some places 40 m high, situated in the middle of Denmark's largest nature and desert area with dunes, heath, and plantation, unbroken from coast to coast. The best starting point for hikers is reached by leaving the main road between Skagen and Frederikshavn by the road towards Kandestederne. After 3 km there is a parking place on the left, at the foot of the peculiar nature phenomenon. These white dunes, which were purchased by the State in 1902 and since then kept free of any vegetation, used to move 8-10 m in a northeasterly direction every year. Now it moves up to about 20 m annually. All together, it has moved about 5 km into the land from the likewise protected stone plain, Råbjerg Stene, in the west. 1,620 hectares have been protected in and around Råbjerg Mile. Adding the protected Hulsig Heath of 2,170 hectares, the protected part of the Grenen peninsula, and Skagen and Bunken Dune Plantations, also state-owned, an area of 62 square kilometres of unique nature has been protected as an untouched nature reserve.

SKAGEN HARBOUR

Apart from the road to Aalbæk to the south, the railway from Frederikshavn, the colony of artists known as the Skagen Painters, and not least all the tourists, Skagen's harbour is the main reason for the growth of the town in the 20th century. The fishing harbour was constructed in 1904-1907 and has expanded many times, initially to provide space for the growing fishing fleet and later for fish industry. Second only to Esbjerg and Thyborøn Skagen is the place, where Danish, respectively foreign fishermen land most fish (120,503 tonnes, respectively 212,354 tonnes, in 2001, the total value of which approaches 700 million DKK, almost 100 million Euro). The fishing port with the characteristic protected warehouses by Thorvald Bindesbøll is still the main attraction of this busy little town.

HIRSHOLMENE

This is a small protected group of islands with many colonies of seagulls and terns on the eastside of the great sand reef stretching some 7 - 8 kilometres out into the Kattegat sea from south west of Frederikshavn. The area totals around 40 hectares. Of the low and stony islets, only the 17 hectares large Hirsholm is inhabited by four humans (2004), a church with a beautiful late Gothic altar piece from approximately 1500, and a lighthouse. The largest islet is Græsholm with 21.5 hectares, to the north east. Other islets are Tyvholm and Kølpen, while the former little islets Kovsholm, Storeholm, Pikkerholm and Dødemand ("Dead Man"), now have coalesced with Græsholm. For centuries, the main activities were fishing and primitive farming, with a little smuggling and looting of shipwrecks added to it, but the picture changed. In the 1700's all male inhabitants lived from fishing and pilot duties. The first lighthouse, now serving as a view tower on top of the old residence of the lighthouse keeper, was built as late as in 1838. The new lighthouse, on top of the highest point of the island, the Ørnebjerg ("Eagles Hill"), was erected in 1882. Many times the wars in the 1600's, 1700's and the beginning of the 1800's actively involved the islands. In 1883 Hirsholmerne were taken over by the government which together with the municipality of Frederikshavn runs the administration of the islands and the boat connection from here to Frederikshavn. There is admittance to Hirsholm only where you may see the alcidae black guillemot by the harbour.

Jetsmark Church

The large and harmonious church building in Jetsmark is looming in the flat landscape south of Pandrup in the Vendsyssel region, northern Jutland. Like many other Danish village churches, it is dedicated to the saint of the sailors and of the children, Saint Nicholas. It was originally built of finely cut granite squares during the Romanesque period according to the classical pattern with an apse, a choir and a nave. What makes the church particularly capturing, is its rich treasure of informative murals. Apart from a few pictures from about 1350 on the northern side of the choir, the amazingly well preserved murals were created in 1474, such as stated in the choir on the rood arch of the western part of the vestry. Among the pictures a doomsday event, where among others, a Pope and a King are driven into jaws of Hell, should be mentioned in particular. The ornamentation from those days are owed to the Bishop of Børglum, Jep Friis, as well as the insertion of a star-ribbed vault in the choir and three cross-ribbed vaults in the nave, while the apse was equipped with a triple ribbed vault separated from the choir as a sacristy. The heavy west tower, made of reused granite squares and medieval bricks, is almost contemporary; so is the late-Gothic porch. Both the Lutheran winged altar piece and the pulpit in early Renaissance are from the end of the 16th century, while the runic stone of the porch, excavated in Pandrup, dates from the 10th century.

ICE WINTER

In spite of the relativly northern position of Denmark on the northern hemisphere, it happens fairly seldom that belts and sounds freeze, apart from the inner waters, such as e.g. Limfjorden in Northern Jutland. Severe ice winters with ice breakers in action characterised the years of 1940, 1941, and 1942, during the Second World War. Subsequently, significant ice winters appeared in 1947, 1963, 1970, 1986, and 1987. Meanwhile, the gradually milder winters have caused the ice breakers, which are held in continuous readiness, to stay almost inactive for several years.

Icebreaker

The icebreaker "Isbjørn", or Ice Bear, its sister ship "Danbjørn", or Dan Bear, both built in 1965, as well as "Thorbjørn", or Thor Bear, built 1980, all pertained to the particular public ice services of the State, until 1996, when the functions were taken over by the Navy

SEMI-DETACHED HOUSES

Semi-detached houses are family-dwellings built together with joint firewalls in between, and usually built in one or two floors, more rarely three. It is a traditional way of building in Danish provincial towns, and since the 1920's semi-detached houses have been a distinctive characteristic in suburbs of most major towns. In 2002 13% of Danes lived in row or semidetached houses.

Hjerl Hede

This special museum is situated in the outskirts of the protected heath Hjerl Hede with the lake Flyndersø, south east of Skive in Jutland. With about 100,000 visitors per year this museum and workshop ranks as one of the most popular attractions in Denmark. While it was opened to the public in 1934, it was made part of the Hjerl Foundation in 1931 which was established in 1915 by the businessman H.P. Hjerl Hansen who bought the area in 1910. It was detached from the foundation in 1979, but has become the main beneficiary of the funds of the foundation. It consists of a number of buildings from old village environments, from Jutland in particular - e.g. farms, mills, an inn, a forge, a dairy, a school, a vicarage, and a replica of a Romanesque church. Furthermore, there are the special sections of the Forestry Museum of Jutland and the Museum of Bog Works. The museum has made a pioneering contribution through active environments such as a working Stone Age settlement, and it has established a framework for various historical experiments, such as Romanesque frescoes and classic cultivation of the moors.

Aalborg

Denmark's fourth largest town has 121,000 inhabitants, while the municipality of Aalborg has 163,000 (2004). The town is located next to Limfjorden, between Himmerland and the original Aalborg (photo, left) and the district of Nørresundby on the northern shore of Limfjorden where the airport is situated. Through many years this city has been known for its aquavit production, its cement and tobacco industry, and its entertainment, in particular in Jomfru Ane Gade and in the summer period at the Tivoliland amusement park and the Aalborg Zoo. At Lindholm Høje, in the northwestern outskirts of Nørrresundby, an old burial ground has been excavated with ceremonial stone-lined ship-settings dating from the 7th century to the late Viking Age and with remnants of a village from 600-1100 AD. First mention of Aalborg was made in 1035 as "Alabu". The oldest part of the cathedral, today's Saint Budolfi Church (picture, slightly above centre) dates back to the middle of the 15th century. The Holy Spirit Monastery, or Aalborg Monastery, was established in 1431, while the "Jens Bang's Stonehouse" was built in 1624. Aalborg has many educational institutions, e.g. the university from 1974 and museums, such as the Museum of Art for Northern Jutland. Among novelties to be mentioned are the Aalborg Congress and Cultural Centre, the Gigantium Sport and Culture Centre, and, probably to be built between 2004-2006, the House of Music by the waterfront.

Hot Air Balloon

The Danish climate is suitable for balloon flying, particularly in the summer. The picture shows a balloon on it way above a summer landscape, - one of the approximately 35 registered balloons in Denmark. Such hot-air balloons partly consist of a container - the balloon itself - and partly of a hamper for the skipper and his passengers. The propulsion is owed to the hot air produced by a propane gas burner placed in the opening in the buttom of the balloon.

FYRKAT

Until now four of the circular Trelleborg-fortresses of the Viking period in Denmark have been found and examined. The smallest one, Fyrkat, southeast of Hobro, was excavated in 1950-1963 and opened to the public in a re-constructed shape in 1959. Today, the Viking Centre Fyrkat consists of the circular fortress with an inner surface of 4.5 hectares, a reconstructed Viking house outside the ramparts, and a reconstructed magnate's farm, which is the centre of various Viking events in the summertime. The thickness of the ramparts is about 12 m and their original height about 3 meters, apart from a stockade supposed to have crowned the ramparts. Each quarter inside the ramparts contained four wooden barracks making a square courtyard. These 16 buildings were built in a bole-house or half-timber technique, each house being 28.5 meters long, equal to 96 Roman feet. The Vikings had their graveyard northeast of the fortification. Fyrkat is supposed to be founded by King Harold Bluetooth in 974-83 according to dendrochonological measures. Before its completion the fortress was destroyed during a battle and completely burnt down, possibly during the fight, which Harold's son, Sweyn Forkbeard, began shortly after his reconquest of the Hedeby region, and which ended with the death of Harold in 986 or 987.

AGRICULTURAL AREAS

Farmland, gardening, grasslands, lawns in urban areas and somewhat uncultivated areas cover some 65% of the total Danish land area of more than 43,000 square kilometres. Today the number of full time farmers is clearly declining. This is mainly due to the merging of smaller farms into agricultural units of considerable size. Consequently, a farming operation may consist of one or more properties. Today approximately 12,000 farmers own 2 or 3 properties. If this trend continues, it is anticipated that in 2010 there will be a total of about 13,500 farms in Denmark, divided into 5,000 cattle breeding farms, 5,750 pig farms and only 2,750 grain growing farms. In 2002 there were about 50,000 farming units in Denmark, almost half of which were growing grain only, while 10,000 were breeding cattle, and 3,500 pigs and poultry. Moreover, the ecologic sector in farming is increasing rapidly. The area used for ecologic cultivation increased by 40% from 2000 to 2001 and now covers about 131,000 hectares, corresponding to almost to 5% of the total agricultural area.

INLET OF MARIAGER

The 1-2 km narrow inlet, at certain places rather resembling a river, cuts some 35 km into northeastern Jutland with the old town of Hobro at the inner end. Even though the inlet has a depth of 28 m there, the mouth and the outer parts of the estuary is extremely shallow. Consequently the 6 m deep sailing canal must be dredged continiously. Larger towns in the neighbourhood are the monastery town, Mariager, on the southern shore and Hadsund on the northern. The last cement factory at the inlet closed down in 1983 as production was centralised in Aalborg, but at the road along the inlet the only Nordic salt factory is located. Here Akzo Nobel Salt A/S produces approx. 600,000 tonnes of various sorts of salt annually. A large part of this is exported to the other Nordic countries.

VIBORG

The well-known cathedral town, with the 2.7 square kilometre Viborg Lake with Nørresø on one side and Søndersø on the other side of the road embankment in between, was already the location of a market and of the provincial thing during the late Iron Age. From 1065 it was a cathedral town, and it was one of the major bases for the south-bound army routes. About 100 years later it was granted its town charter and privileges. Before the Reformation in 1536 the fortified town had some 10 churches and no less than 5 monastic orders, and it was also hosting many noblemen's assemblies. Then a recession followed, increased by wars, plagues and many town fires, the most violent of which took place in 1726. The town returned to glory and dignity when hosting the Assembly of the Estates of Northern Jutland 1836-1848 and had a further upturn due to the cultivation of the moors and the development of the railroad. Today, the town of Viborg has 33,000 inhabitants, while the municipality has 43,000 inhabitants, many trade activities and a variety of industries. It is an important administration and institution town, hosting the Western High Court, the Provincial Archives for Northern Jutland, the Viborg County Governor's Office, the Viborg County Mayor's Office, the head office of the biggest Danish agricultural consultants, Det Danske Hedeselskab, the congress and music hall, Tinghallen, the Viborg Provincial Historical Museum, and Skovgaard Museet i Viborg. The present cathedral, however, was built as late as 1864-1876 as a reconstruction of the Roman church from the 12th and 13th century.

THE WORLD MAP IN KLEJTRUP

The almost circular Klejtrup Lake in the village of Klejtrup, about 10 km south east of Hobro, Jutland, is widely known for its World Map. The 50 x 100 m large world atlas with countries, lakes, rivers and mountain chains, built of earth and stone, was established by Søren Poulsen (1888-1969) in 1944-1969 and is a popular tourist attraction. In the middle of the picture is Africa, to the left North and Latin America, north of Africa is Europe and to the right, at the upper eastern part, Asia and below Australia. As the closest neighbour to the world-map the huge Klejtrup Voldsted with its two hills is situated. Unfortunately no remnants or traces of walls have been found which could indicate the time of the construction. South-west of the farm Brattingsborg, there is another rampart known as Klejtrup Walls. Tradition has it that Inge, the son of King Niels, was kicked to death at Klejtrup in 1121. Another story goes that Ingrid, the wife of Henrik, grandson of King Sweyn Estridson, fled from Klejtrup with her lover. He was eventually captured, brought back to King Niels at Klejtrup and buried alive. Nor is it possible to date these ramparts.

FRIJSENBORG

There is no admittance to the palace-like manor house of one of the largest estates in Denmark, Frijsenborg, west of Århus in Jutland. Its present appearance of a dynastic look was achieved only in the last peak period of the great families at the end of the 19th century, when Christian Emil Count Krag-Juel-Vind-Frijs, abbreviated to C.E. Frijs, and subsequently his son, Mogens Count Krag-Juel-Vind-Frijs, resided here, as some of the largest landowners in the country. The history of Frijsenberg begins with the small village manor Jernit north of the village Hammel. Later, the main building from the 1580's was renovated and extended in the 1690's and totally reconstructed 1862-1882, inspired by French, English and Dutch manorial architecture, and furnished for C.E. Frijs with precious materials provided by the architect Ferdinand Meldahl. From 1923, Frijsenborg has been in the hands of the Wedell family, from 1958 it was managed in joint ownership with the large estate Wedellsborg on western Funen. The forestry is managed under the name of Wefri A/S. All together, the two agricultural and forestry estates represent more than 9,600 hectares, of which almost 6,600 hectares are forests.

SKAFØGÅRD

At the end of the 19th century Denmark was from time to time virtually ruled from Skaføgaard. At that time the prime minister Jacob Brønnum Scavenius Estrup was the land owner at this three-winged manor in eastern Jutland. Estrup was the firm head of government from 1875 till 1894, from 1885 almost as a dictator , as he ruled the country ignoring the parliamentary majority of Liberals, assisted by his mounted gendarmes. Skaføgård was initially a farming village called Skaby. The present estate was established by the royal council member Jørgen Ottosen Rosenkrantz, who had the Renaissance manor house and the farm yard constructed, each on their islet, in the years 1580-1582. Today the manor house, surrounded by moats, appears as one of the country's most complete manor constructions of the French style. The characteristic gate house was added about 1600. J.B.S. Estrup bought Skaføgård in 1852. In connection with a renovation 1856-1857, he added the protruding entrance in the middle of the court yard. Skaføgård is still in the possession of the descendants of the prime minister, along with the property called Højholt. The forest is managed as a limited company. Including forests, cottages, farms and fields, the estate covers 999 hectares.

THE FRIGATE "JYLLAND"

The old man-of-war, the propeller frigate "Jylland", has always been up against the winds, thus in the autumn 2003, when it appeared that the ship was to be fully embedded, only allowing the masts to be seen. "Jylland", launched in 1860, the last great warship built in oak wood, achieved immortal honours in the battle of Heligoland against the allied Austrian-Prussian squadron on the 9th of May, 1864, even if the victory had no decisive effect on the outcome of the war. Its armament consisted of 44 heavy front loaded guns, and the crew was counting 430 men. Five times did "Jylland" sail to the Danish Virgin Islands. After its last cruise on active duty, during which the Danish-born and future King Haakon VII of Norway participated as voluntary apprentice, "Jylland" served for some time as a floating barrack at Holmen in Copenhagen. It was also in private ownership for a numer of years. In 1960 the 76 meter long hull of the frigate was towed to Ebeltoft in eastern Jutland, where it was placed in the merchant harbour as a public museum. In 1989-1994 the ship was thoroughly renovated with financial support from the A.P. Møller Foundation. The number of paying visitors amounts to approximately 120,000 annually.

KALØ CASTLE RUINS

To be able to reach the remote ruin on its islet in the bottom of Kalø Bay, you have to climb a 500 m long paved embankment which supposedly dates back to the construction of the castle by Erik VI Menved around 1314. So is the round corner tower to the north, part of the ring-wall, a sally gate, and the remains of another tower, next to the 10 m high core tower, with up to 3 m thick walls. Originally the core tower was 14 m high. The great tower was most probably built by Count Gerhard III or by the Holstein nobleman, Claus Limbek, to whom the Count had pledged Kalø. The circular, eastern corner tower and perhaps the entire keep has been added during the reign of King Valdemar IV Atterdag. It may have happened after his acquisition of Northern Jutland in 1343, when he may have appointed Claus Limbek his captain at Kalø Castle. Up to 1660 Kalø was the seat of a royal vassal and also served as a state prison, i.a. for the Swedish king-to-be, Gustav Wasa in 1518-1519. Gradually the once so impressive fortress lost its military importance and fell into decay, and in 1672 it was torn down. The first excavations of the ruin, nowadays protected, commenced in 1903, and from the 1920's until approximately 1945 the National Museum of Denmark was in charge of the excavations and renovation works.

THE PADDLE STEAMER "HJEJLEN"

Further to all the spectacular sceneries, the beautiful area around the hill Himmelbjerget has a tourist attraction in Denmark's oldest existing passenger ship, the paddle steamer "Hjejlen". Along with the other sight-seeing boats of the steamship company, every summer it shuttles between Himmelbjerget and the town of Silkeborg, where it lands at Langebro. The steamship was built in 1861 in the shipyard of Baumgarten & Burmeister, later Burmeister & Wain, in Copenhagen. The ship is 25.7 m long. It has a gross deadweight of 39 tonnes and is powered by a two-cylinder steam engine, consuming 100 kg coal per hour, allowing for a speed of 8 knots. Apart from some minor repairs, adjustments and renovations, "Hjejlen" remains the same ship cruising on the Silkeborg lakes, as when originally making her maiden voyage attended by Frederick VII.

ÅRHUS

Since the appearance of Århus in 10th century, the city has become Denmark's second largest town with about 291,000 inhabitants in the municipality and about 223,000 in the city itself. It has its own parallel to the Tivoli Gardens in Copenhagen, Tivoli Friheden (Tivoli Freedom) and, furthermore, Denmark's only chartered town museum, several theatres, its own opera house, own city orchestra, museums of international standard, its own university, and the gigantic town festival, Århus Festuge. Also, Århus has the longest cathedral in Denmark (in the centre of the picture). It is 93 m long and its gross area covers 3,070 square meters. It was established in the first part of the 13th century and is probably the third cathedral in the history of the city. During a major reconstruction from the beginning of the 15th century lasting until around 1480, it was modified into High Gothic style and largely received its present appearance with its 92 m high tower. It contains some of the country's most magnificent fresco decorations, many of them derived from the big reconstruction before 1480. Other sights are the huge altar piece of Bernt Notke, donated to the cathedral in 1479, the two rows of choir chairs from 1508, the brass baptismal font from 1481, the rood arch crucifix from the end of the 15th century, the masterly made pulpit in high Renaissance style from 1588 and not less than 41 commemorative tablets and about 80 gravestones.

LÆSØ

Visitors arrive to Vesterø Harbour on the north-west side of the island of Læsø, when the trip is made by the little ferry boat from Frederikshavn in Northern Jutland. Østerby Havn in the north-east is the most important fishing harbour, particularly for Norway lobster fishing. Yet, none of the towns are big. In the Vesterø Harbour, where a Maritime and Fishery Museum was opened in 1976, there were 481 permanent inhabitants, by 2003; in Østerby Harbour they were 337, while the main town of the island, Byrum, with the Læsø Museum Farm House, the number of inhabitants amounts to 458. However, it is estimated that more than half of the approx. 200,000 passengers from the ferry boats are tourists, who arrive here either to spend a summer day on the island, or to spend their holidays in one of the hotels or guesthouses, or in one of the roughly 850 summer houses. The island covers 101 square kilometres. It is not least the exciting nature and the rich bird life, which has a magnetic attraction on the many tourists. In spite of its modest size and its only 2,200 inhabitants, Læsø still constitutes an independent municipality in the County of North Jutland.

LANGØRE

The little charming fishing village Langøre, or Langør, is situated on a point which was formerly an island. It reaches from north down towards the firth of Stavns Fjord, full of islands, on the east coast of the island of Samsø. Today a narrow embankment leads to the fjord. The harbour was constructed during the wars against the English, 1807-1814, and east of the harbour remnants of an almost ruined entrenchment from the time can still be seen. Furthermore, large storehouses, a gun boat station, and barracks were built. Soon, the harbour became the most important shipping facility of Samsø and business was flourishing, but after the mid-1800's the harbour faded out and lost its importance. Instead, some fishermen settled in order to develop the inlet fishing, but their days are almost gone, too. Langøre, on the other hand, has changed its character and now appears a true Mecca for the numerous pleasure boats which are harbouring at this peaceful spot from where the gun boats launched their raids in 1809 to border the English warships.

HIMMELBJERGET

Popularly, Himmelbjerget, "the Sky Mountain", in the beautiful surroundings near Julsø, 11 km south-east of Silkeborg in Jutland, was long considered the highest point, not only in the hilly Silkeborg area, but in all of Denmark, also long time after surveys of the General Staff had given the honour to Ejer Bavnehøj in the lake upland south of the large Mossø lake, also in Jutland. Sky Mountain measures 147 m and is crowned by a 25 m high watch tower, inaugurated in 1875 in honour of King Frederick VII. Ejer Bavnehøj, which is 170 m high on its own, and, including a tower on the top, 184 m, was then considered the highest point in Denmark until 1943. For the nearby Yding Skovhøj actually measures almost 173 m, but like Ejer Bavnehøj it is artificially enlarged, by a burial mound. In reality the highest natural point in the country is the spruceclad Møllehøj of 170 m, located south-west of Ejer Bavnehøj. Back to Sky Mountain. After all, it is a so-called 'false' hill, i.e. an erosion cliff at the edge of a moraine plateau in the Mid-Jutland lake upland. It is a very popular excursion venue, with several memorial stones, e.g. for the politician A. F. Tscherning, the great leader of Inner Mission, Vilhelm Beck, and the poet priest, Steen Steensen Blicher, who arranged large public gatherings here in the years 1839-45.

HEE CHURCH

Hee Church, east of the dike of Stadil Fjord inlet in western Jutland is not a representative Danish village church, but never the less considered to be one of the most magnificent Romanesque constructions on Danish soil. The otherwise rather simple building, raised in the middle of the 12th century by granite quadrants, received its peculiar, richly ornamented west tower at the end of the same century, probably because it also functioned as a shire assembly house. It did so until the end of the 17th century. Unfortunately it was restored in a rather crude manner in 1882-1884, when the upper part of the tower was replaced and the entire peculiar western part was torn down, while the late Gothic extensions (picture, left) were "normalized" into Romanesque style. Apart from the bevel base underneath the choir and the nave, very few details from the time of the foundation more than 800 years ago have been saved. In the church there is an altar piece in late Renaissance style from 1635, a late Gothic parish clerk's chair from about 1550, a richly ornamented parish clerk's chair in high Renaissance style from about 1600, master chairs from 1655, and a Romanesque granite font with sepals, of the western Jutland type. The liberal politician J.C. Christensen (1856-1930), who was the head of government from 1905 to 1908, is buried in the graveyard.

CLAUSHOLM

Few Danish manors have been associated with so much dramatic love, as this stately Baroque residence south-east of Randers in the middle of the East-Jutland manor landscape. This is the story of the infatuated King Frederick IV's abduction from this castle of the young Anna Sophie, daughter of the Great Chancellor Conrad Reventlow. The absolute king had met the beautiful and lively girl at a masquerade at Skanderborg Castle and had fallen passionately in love. He married her to his left hand, and the day after the funeral of his Queen Louise in 1721 to his right hand. The affair aroused much attention, and immediately upon the king's death in 1730 Anna Sophie was banished to Clausholm, where she lead a quiet life until her death in 1743. Clausholm has been known since the 1300s. The present three-winged manor house was erected in 1693-1701 by Conrad Reventlow, but the H-shape of today is owed to the two small wings added by King Frederick IV in 1722-23. In 1800 the manor was bought by Hans Heinrich Friccius von Schilden, whose descendents still own it. There is public admittance to the beautifully furnished manor house in July, while the large castle park with the active fountains stays open from May 1st to September 30th. Occasionally, concerts are held in the great hall, as well as special exhibitions and various arrangements.

JELLING

The municipality of Jelling has only 5,700 inhabitants (2004) and of those 2,900 in the town. It is the only town and station of some size along the Vejle-Give railroad line. Jelling is mainly known for its monuments, consisting of fragments of a huge ceremonial ship-setting of stones and for the two Mounds of Jelling, made in 958-959 and in the 970's AD. The oldest one, the North Hill to the right of the church has a diameter of 65 m, while the South Hill on the other side of the church has a diameter of 77 m. The 11 m high burial mounds are the largest ones in Denmark. There are indications that Queen Thyra was buried in the North Hill and her husband, King Gorm, in the South Hill. To the monuments also belong three runic stones from the Viking period. One is the Small Stone of Jelling, or the Stone of Gorm, from the first half of the 900's, the other is The Great Stone of Jelling, which was erected by King Harold Bluetooth, for his parents, Gorm and Thyra, in the second part of the 900's. The two runic stones are placed in front of the porch of the church. In 1964 small fragments of a third runic stone were found. Underneath the floor in the Romanesque church from about 1100 traces of not less than three burnt down wooden churches have been found. In 1978 a chamber grave with the remains of a man's skeleton, possibly Gorm's, whom the christened Harold might have transferred to the church, was also found. The history of Jelling can be studied more closely in the exhibition centre, "Kongernes Jelling" - The Kings' Jelling -, opened in 2000.

BILLUND AIRPORT

Since the introduction of the Great Belt connection, the domestic air traffic has been reduced at the Airport of Billund, but the international traffic is increasing. The airport opened on the moor northeast of Billund in 1964, following the extension two years before of the landing strip established by the toy manufacturer LEGO for their own aircrafts. In 1997 the airport was reorganised and turned into a limited liability company, with the previous partners, Vejle County and the municipalities of Kolding, Vejle, Billund, Grindsted, and Give as the shareholders. It is today the second largest airport in the country and continuously expanding, so as to be able to handle all types of modern civilian aircrafts.

LEGOLAND

LEGOLAND, the famous amusement park, with 1.6 million visitors (2003), located in Billund, between Vejle and Grindsted, in the centre of western Jutland, is one of the most popular tourist attractions in Denmark. It was established in 1968 by the toy manufacturer LEGO (now the LEGO Group) and is constructed of LEGO toy bricks, like a miniature country with copies of famous buildings, cities, and vessels, etc., in the scale of 1:20. It has been supplemented with a Wild West town, a traffic school for children, moving entertainment attractions, a museum for puppets and mechanical toys. The first LEGOLAND abroad was opened in Windsor in England in 1996. A third LEGOLAND Park in Carlsbad in California opened in 1999 and in 2002 was followed by a fourth one in Günzburg in Southern Germany.

OIL RIG

On the whole Denmark was completely dependent of imported oil until 1972, when the exploitation of oil and natural gas was commenced in the Danish share of the North Sea. Since 1997 the country has been self-supplying with energy, and today the production is considerably larger than the domestic consumption. Natural gas is being exported to Sweden and Germany, while the surplus oil production primarily is sold on the spot market. The A. P. Møller Group is the largest Danish producer in the North Sea.

ESBJERG

Today Esbjerg is the fifth largest city district in Denmark with 72,000 inhabitants in the town and 82,300 in the municipality (2004). The modern metropolis of the western part of Jutland has experienced a rather remarkable growth by Danish standards, since the politicians in 1868 decided to build a port in a place only occupied by two farms. Since then Esbjerg has become a transport, trade and regional centre with an airport, a heliport, a ferry, fishery and leasure boat harbour, with higher educational institutions and facilities. The large harbour has maritime links to Fanø, Harwich in England, Bergen in Norway, and Thorshavn on the Faroe Islands. The role which fish for human consumption played to the employment and the economy, has been taken over by the offshore activities in connection with the oil and natural gas extraction from the North Sea. Some of the remarkable novelties in and around this enterprising town are the Fishery and Maritime Museum, and the Esbjerg Museum of Art, which reopened in 1977 having been rebuilt as an attachment to the new Music Hall of Esbjerg; furthermore, the four 15 m high sculptures of white concrete, "People by the seaside", made by the sculptor Svend Wiig Hansen, at Sædding, north of the town. In 2003 a project to build a 125 m high tower with 33 floors next to the harbour was proposed. The building which will become the tallest in Denmark will include a hotel and a restaurant, offices, and representative facilities.

POWER PLANT

The power plant company Vestkraft A/S runs the Esbjerg Plant, situated in the southern outskirts of Esbjerg, and four de-centralised power-heating plants. In 2000 Vestkraft A/S was purchased by Elsam A/S along with six other power plant companies in Jutland and on Funen.

SCULPTURES

In 1995 Esbjerg got its new landmark, when the enormous sculpture group " People at the Seaside " by the sculptor, painter and graphic designer, Svend Wiig Hansen, was unveiled in the suburb Sædding, north of the town. The four 15 m high figures, sitting down, bending backwards, with their eyes directed towards the sea, are made of white concrete and appear as a provoking meeting between humans and nature, and between nature and culture. However, probably the provocation is primarily due to the size of the sculptures. Svend Wiig Hansen may have been inspired by the Greek Bronze Age art of the archipelago of the Cyclades and from the famous giant statues on the Easter Islands in the south-eastern Pacific.

CATHEDRAL OF HADERSLEV

The tall choir (in front) with the big flying buttresses of the cathedral in the old town Haderslev in southern Jutland, towers dominantly above the mainly old surrounding buildings and is considered by many to be the most beautiful Gothic construction in the country, a true masterpiece. The cathedral is dedicated to Our Lady and consists of sections from several different periods. The oldest part is the transept from about 1250. The long triple nave is a little younger, from approximately 1270, and the impressive choir construction is from about 1420. The side chapels are from the late Middle Ages, the front hall to the west was built in 1650, while the sacristy and the porch are of much younger age. The western tower of the cathedral disappeared in 1627, when the troops of the German General Wallenstein burned down the town during the Thirty Years' War. In spite of all intensions it was never rebuilt. The cathedral had a predecessor, a church in granite from the middle of the 12th century, while no traces of an even older wooden building have been found. The church contains late Gothic frescoes, a baptismal font cast in bronze in 1485, a pulpit from 1636 and two burial vaults with 13 distinguished funeral paintings. The church became a cathedral when the diocese of Haderslev was established in 1922. Until the Reformation in 1536 it was both a parish church and a subsidiary of the cathedral in Schleswig with a chapter of Benedictine monks.

RIBE

Close to the tidal area Vadehavet in the south-west of Jutland, Ribe is the oldest genuine town in Denmark. It dates back to the 8th century. Around 860, Ansgar, the "Apostle of the North", built a church in the town which became a bishop's residence already in 948. Ribe received its town charter in the early 1200s. Through the Middle Ages Ribe was a centre for shipping and trade, thus expanding to the west bank of the small Ribe river, where its new town centre and the colossal cathedral (picture, centre right) was constructed about 1150-1250. Outside the old town is the 8 m high castle bank with its rampart and remains of the old royal fortress of Riberhus. After the Reformation in 1536 the town stagnated and as the trading routes changed and the river sanded up in the middle of the 17th century, the great era was over. Ribe only regained prosperity after Southern Jutland's reunion with Denmark in 1920. Today the town has about 8,000 inhabitants, while the municipality of Ribe has about 18,000 inhabitants. Apart from being the center of the diocese and of the municipality, the town is also the site of the Ribe County Mayor's office and of the Ribe County Governor's office. Historical enthusiasts will benefit from visiting the old part of town, with its intact medieval street structure and the many well-preserved half-timbered and stone houses from the 15th and 17th centuries, or museums like "The Vikings of Ribe", and "The Ribe Viking centre" about 2 km to the south.

MARSH

Sometimes the landscape may achieve the most extraordinary shapes, such as these small islands in a lake, south of Esbjerg, which rather resemble cartoon figures. Digging for turf often created conspicuous landscapes with lakes ideal for many freshwater fish like pike, perch, carp and eel, and for birds like mallard, teal, wigeon, and shoveler. Marshes, such as those depicted, may be almost inundated by grey geese and Canadian geese on their way north in the Spring. Marshes are also a favorite habitat of the small and fast flying snipe, the hopeful target of any keen shot. If these birds escaped the lead pellets of their shooting predators, they might still suffer from lead poisoning by swallowing the pellets, which had landed in the marshes and in the tidal areas, according to the experts. Consequently, this biotope was protected by a ban on lead pellets in the 1980's. Today lead shots are forbidden all over the country, and pellets of steel and wolfram, or tungsten, are used in stead. The remaining marshes are also protected against cultivation, partly by the law, partly by the economic development: cultivation does not pay off, anymore, with the present grain prices and production limitations.

RØMØ

The long very wide sand beaches near Lakolk on the west coast of the island Rømø west of Southern Jutland are among the finest in Europe. Every summer approximately 2-2.5 million tourists visit the island which measures almost 129 square kilometres and has a permanent population of approx. 730 inhabitants (2004). The island is reached by the 9.2 km long and 6 m high Rømø embankment. It was built in 1939-1948 and starts west of Skærbæk on the west coast of Southern Jutland and attaches to Rømø at Nørre Tvismark. Rømø is one of the North Frisian Islands, which shelter the North Sea coast all the way from Esbjerg in Denmark down to the mouth of the great river, the Elb, in Germany; the Frisian islands continue along the north coast of Germany and Holland as the East Frisian Islands and only stop short of Amsterdam with the West Frisian Islands. Originally they constituted the continental coastline, but through deluges in the Middle Ages the sea isolated these fertile islands from their motherlands by vast tidal areas. The special old Frisian dialect spoken by the Frisian tribes still survives in the Dutch and German Frieslands and in part of west Schleswig, especially in the coastal country south of the Danish-German border.

MIDSUMMER EVE BONFIRE

According to popular belief the 23rd of June, the evening before the birthday of St. John the Baptist, was a one of special powers. It was believed that medicinal herbs collected in this night were more powerful and that the dew on the grass had curative effects, as had the water in the holy springs. Therefore, numerous pilgrims made it to the springs on this evening and night, thus giving rise to the so-called spring markets with their entertainers, tents and booths. One reminiscence of this time is the the amusement park Dyrehavsbakken, next to Kirsten Pil's Spring north of Copenhagen. To chase out the evil forces during that powerful night, when witches were said to be passing by on their flying broomsticks on their way to gathering places in Bloksbjerg (Brocken in the Harz) and Hekkenfeldt on Iceland, bonfires were built in high places and barrels of tar and poles with straw-bundles were set on fire. Today's tradition of lighting a bonfire at dusk that evening and to place a witch-like figure on top of it, while the crowd sings the midsummer song of the poet Holger Drachmann from his adventure comedy "Once upon a time", composed in 1885, first became popular during the 20th century. Around the country speeches are held by politicians or artists.

SCHACKENBORG

No less than three times in recent years this manor within the village Møgeltønder in the western part of Southern Jutland has attracted more than ordinary attention. The first time was in 1993, when Prince Joachim, the youngest son of H.M. Queen Margrethe, officially received the property. It was already offered to him in 1978 by the last member and childless owner of the Schack family, with the actual transfer scheduled to take place in 1993, when the prince was expected to have accomplished his agricultural studies. The second time was in connection with the prince's wedding to the present Princess Alexandra in 1995, when a substantial public donation was used mainly to renovate the old manor house. The third time was in 2002, when the second son of the couple, Prince Felix, was baptized amidst a massive media attention in the spacious church of Møgeltønder, the history of which dates back to the Middle Ages, like that of Schackenborg. The eldest son, Prince Nicolai, was baptized in the church of Fredensborg Castle. The first time the manor was mentioned was in 1223. Soon after it was called Møgeltønderhus. In 1661 it was acquired by the field marshal Hans Schack, who had the present manor buildings constructed in 1662 – 1666. The manor remained in the possession of the Schack family until the take-over by Prince Joachim, who had accomplished, by then, his military and agricultural educations in Denmark and abroad.

FLOWER FIELD

Fields full of flowers break the monotony of the many grain and grass fields in the open landscape. The return on the Danish gardening industry amounts to approximately 4 billion DKK annually. The most important export markets for plants are Germany and Sweden. The major part of these exports consists of flowers and potted plants.

RIDING AT THE RING

This is a kind of horse back riding competition, where the rider with his lance endeavours to pierce and seize a metal ring hanging down from a so-called gallows. The riders compete about piercing most rings, and they are galloping for the ring several times each. The rider, who seizes most rings, is appointed the "Ring Riding King" and is crowned with a wreath. The tradition originates from the tournaments of the knights in the Middle Ages and was called "Ring Running" or "Carrousel" as a valued entertainment at the European royal courts in the 16th-18th centuries, i.a. during the famous Christian IV. The tradition is still maintained between May and September across Southern Jutland, from where this photograph from Aabenraa was taken, but also in other places, like Bornholm, in connection with the Shrovetide celebrations.

THE CASTLE OF SØNDERBORG SLOT

The largest town of Southern Jutland, with some 27,000 inhabitants in the town and about 30,000 in the municipality (2004), grew up around the old castle next to the sound of Als Sund (in the lower part of the picture) and the older housing near the waterfront between the castle and the Bridge of Christian X connecting the two city parts on both sides of the sound. Sønderborg is an old maritime town which was granted town privileges in 1461. However, it suffered badly under the bombardments during the war in 1864. The church Sankt Marie Kirke (Holy Mary) at the right of the bridge dates back, in its present shape, to a reconstruction made in 1595-1600. The Castle, meanwhile, has a much longer history. Its year of foundation is supposedly 1169 – contemporary with Absolon's castle in Copenhagen. However, it has been expanded and modified many times since then, i.a. in the mid-1200's, in the first part of the 1400's, in 1550-1570, and in 1718-26, when it was all transformed into Baroque. Last time it was renovated was in 1964-1973. Archaeological excavations are still taking place outside, whereby the north-eastern stronghold of the keep from just after 1500 has been revealed. The castle, now hosting the archaeological and national history Museum of Sønderborg Castle, is probably best known as the state prison for the dethroned King Christian II in 1532-1549. Today, Sønderborg is a town of institutions and of education, first of all. The town is also famous for its annual 'riding at the ring' tournaments in the midsummer, an unparallelled town festival lasting several days. The ship next to the Castle is the royal yacht "Dannebrog".

THE FRØSLEV CAMP

Next to the Danish-German border the German internment camp, Frøslevlejren, was established in 1944. The purpose on the Danish part was to bring back Danes from the notorious German concentration camps to this camp and to see a German promise to stop future deportations to Germany materialised. Deportations had increased strongly following the resignation of the government and the sinking of the Danish Navy on the 29th of August, 1943. The Germans were persuaded to accept, on the condition that the Danish internment camp would be located next to the border. At its peak, the occupancy was 5,460 prisoners, but in spite of a promise not to deport more prisoners to Germany, 1,600 prisoners were transferred from Frøslev to Germany from October, 1944, to February, 1945. Including the prisoners on their way to or back from Germany, the number of prisoners reached 12,000-13,000 during the camp's only nine months of operation. After the liberation of Denmark in May 1945 the camp was transformed into an internment camp for people accused of collaborating during the occupation of Denmark and renamed the Faarhus Camp. In 1949, it was turned over to the Armed Forces and called Padborglejren. Later, it was used by the Air Force, the Medical Corps and finally the Civil Defence Force. Today the Museum of Frøslevlejren is located in the central watchtower and in the former prison barracks H 4 and H 6. Other barracks serve various purposes, such as a nature college, Amnesty International, the UN Museum of the Blue Berets and a continuation school.

Egeskov

This manor is situated on the island of Funen, 16 km north of the town of Svendborg. The present manor house was completed in 1554 as a double-house raised on poles in a lake. It is one of the most impressive manors in the country, with its two corner towers, its stair case tower, and its many loopholes, and, incidentally, the only preserved complex of its kind. First mention was in 1405, when it belonged to the Skinkel family, who remained here until 1545, as it accrued to Frands Brockenhuus, later the Marshal of the Realm. Brockenhuus had the stately and fascinating Renaissance castle built, which we see today, probably with Martin Bussert as the architect, known from Nyborg Castle and Hesselager Manor. Since 1784 Egeskov has been in the possession of the descendants of the royal conference councillor, Henrik Bille-Brahe. Today, the knight's hall is used for concerts and other cultural arrangements. However, first of all it is the castle park of 16 hectares, which every year attracts some 200,000 visitors from near and far. The park contains a Renaissance garden, a Baroque garden, the English park, the world's largest bamboo labyrinth designed by Piet Hein, as well as the Egeskov Veteran Car Museum, the Motor Cycle Museum, the Horse Carriage and Agricultural Museum, the Falck Rescue Service museum, etc. The manor house itself was restored again in 1987.

HVIDKILDE

The beautiful situation, surrounded by forests and small lakes, and facing the road between Fåborg and Svendborg, makes the white Hvidkilde, with the black, glazed tiles, one of the pearls among the many manors of South Funen. Around the middle of the 1500s Eiler Rønnow built the Renaissance castle, which still constitutes the core in this three-winged Baroque manor house, which was completed in 1742. Earlier, this may have been crown land, but among families, which have resided here, are such prominent ones as Bille, Gyldenstjerne, and Gøye. Since 1725, when Hvidkilde was acquired by Johan Lehn, the estate has been owned by his descendents, who are now called Ahlefeldt-Laurvig-Lehn. There is admittance to the park only upon permission, but anyone is free to enjoy the harmonious manor complex from the road.

ROSENSKJOLD

A manor house under construction, now, in the beginning of the 21th century, may appear somewhat anachronistic, but never the less an apparent reality. The castle-like country house, facing the inlet Tybrind Vig on western Funen was built by the cosmetician Heidi Sommer, who made her childhood dream, to have her own castle, come true. Heidi Sommer was quite fascinated by this place, the temperature of which makes it ideal for the cultivation of ecologic roses to be used in producing night creams. Hence the name Rosenskjold ("Rose Shield"). She bought the land and started building the dream palace from her childhood drawings. The first turf was cut in 1992, but the great hall of 600 square metres was not ready until 2002. The inside decoration of Rosenskjold with gold leaf ornaments took place in 1998-2003. There are also plans to decorate the two towers of the building with a layer of gold leaf. Today, Rosenskjold is functioning partly as the estate office of the old estate Bjørnemose, east of Svendborg, also owned by Mrs. Sommer, partly as the head office of her chain of private schools in several Danish and foreign towns. There is no admittance to Rosenskjold. Worth mentioning is that a red buoy indicates the finding place in Tybrind Vig of the oldest stone age settlement, so far, excavated under water. Carbon-14 tested oar blades are dated from the time of the so-called Ertebølle Culture, about 4100 b.C.

FALSLED

The little skippers' village, Falsled, at the bay of Helsnæs on the southwest part of Funen, is protected by the peninsula of Helnæs and by Horne Land in the south. The beautiful, thatched, half-timbered farms of the village lie side by side with the imposing captains' and skippers' houses. Today this picturesque and amazingly well-preserved harbour is not any longer being visited by yachts, galleasses and schooners, but rather by pleasure boats. Although navigation with the proud sailing vessels became uneconomical towards 1900, this pearl, beautifully situated between the estates of Damsbo and Steensgård, with its exclusive manor lodging, is still an appreciated tourist attraction with beaches and forest. For the well-off visitors there is also the inn. However, the inn, too, has undergone great changes, with a past - although not particularly well-documented - as a smugglers' inn as far back as in the 15th century, and later as an ordinary country pub. Today the Falsled Inn definitely has one of the country's best kitchens, well-known in Denmark, as well as abroad. The inn received its very exclusive touch during the years when the film-maker Sven Grønløkke was the owner together with the French born culinary artist Jean-Louis Lieffroy who is still here to the delight of numerous gourmets.

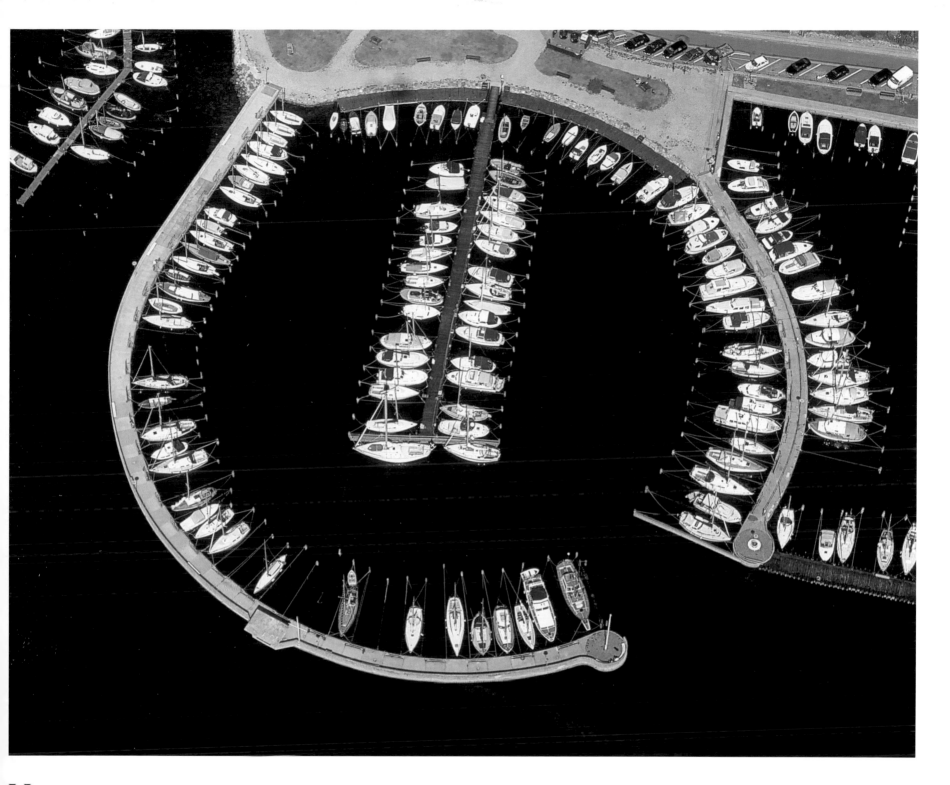

MARINA

Denmark has been a maritime nation since ancient times. Certainly those ships are known, by which the Vikings, also known as the Norse, crossed the great seas to settle down abroad, to trade, and to loot. Nowadays things happen more peacefully, when Danish sailors and shipbuilders prove their skills in the shape of ferries, tankers, container carriers and other merchantmen. The increased spare time and standard of living has resulted in a constant growth in the number of pleasure boats with or without sails, the purpose of which, when disregarding certain large sea races, is generally anything but commercial. In 2002 305 Danish marinas had about 53,000 permanent berths. Danish pleasure sailors accounted for 50% of the over-night stays, Germans for 32%, and Swedes for 10%. The remaining beds were occupied by mainly Dutchmen and Norwegians. Most of the marinas are located in beautiful surroundings, along the many coasts of the country. They offer a variety of services.

HOLCKENHAVN

Holckenhavn, the magnificent four wing Renaissance manor south of Nyborg, is named after Eiler Baron Holck, for whom and for whose posterity the Barony of Holckenhavn was established in 1672. The barony was abolished in 1921, but the old Holck family is still in possession of Holckenhavn. In the 14th century the manor was called Kogsbølle; in 1584 it was called Ulfeldtsholm after the royal councillor Jacob Ulfeldt, and subsequently Ellensborg, after the mother-in-law of King Christian IV, the authoritative and wealthy landowner, Ellen Marsvin, who bought the estate in 1616 and added in 1662-1672 Nygård. The oldest part of the present castle consists of the northern and the eastern wings, which were erected as an angular construction in the years 1579-1585. The tall, square bell tower with its slim spire in front of the courtyard facade of the eastern wing was erected in the years after 1597. Later the wing linking the tower and the northern wing with the most northern part of the eastern wing facing the courtyard, was erected. The proud manor received its final shape in 1631 when Ellen Marsvin built the 50 m long west wing with its beautifully ornamented chapel. Amongst the treasures of Holckenhavn the estate registry book of Jacob Ulfeldt from 1588 should be mentioned, with its colourful documentation of his various properties. It was Jacob Ulfeldt who moved the manor to its present location. Visits by private groups may be arranged (phone: +45 65313105), with guided tours to the chapel, the great hall and the park of 12 hectares.

LINDØVÆRFTET

The largest shipyard in Denmark, Lindøværftet, was established in 1957-1959 near Munkebo northeast of the city of Odense on the island of Funen. It belongs to the A.P. Moeller Group. Its proper name is Odense Staalskibsværft A/S, Lindø. The number of employees is over 8,000, and the annual turnover amounts to billions of DKR (approximately 1.3 billion Euro). Originally the group consisted of two shipping companies listed on the stock exchange, DS 1912 and DS Svendborg. Both were founded by the shipowner mr. A. P. Møller (1876-1965). After his death his son, mr. Mærsk Mc-Kinney Møller, took over and gradually expanded the shipping business, the shipyard, and other widely diversified companies, such as off-shore activities with drilling and extraction of oil and gas from the North Sea as well as big shopping centers in Denmark and abroad. Today the container shipping company Maersk Sealand is the world's largest . Not until the end of 2003 did mr. Maersk Mc-Kinney Møller, 90 years old, officially retire as the chairman of the board of his company, which is Denmark's largest.

Marstal

The combined fishing, pleasure-boat and ferry harbour Marstal is located at the southeast peak of Ærø island, facing the archipelago south of Funen. The town is well protected towards the south and the open Bay of Marstal by the narrow, curved land tongue, Ærøs Hale, to the right in the picture. Originally, Marstal was an insignificant fishing harbour, but the flourishing fishing activities in the early 1700s and the strong expansion of the merchant navy a century later resulted in a strong boom to this skippers' town. Nowadays, it is not the proud, characteristic three-masted Marstal schooners, which dominate the traditional harbour environment, but rather pleasure boats and to some extent coasters. The church was built in 1737-38 by the skippers of Marstal, who freighted the building materials with their own vessels. The old skippers also posed as models for the apostles of the altar piece. The town with its narrow streets and old, close houses, still has a navigation school and a marine museum, as well as a ferry connection to Rudkøbing on the Langeland island. In 1966 one of the largest solar collectors in the world was opened at the outskirts of the town. In 2003 the town of Marstal had approximately 2,300 inhabitants and the municpality a bit less than 3,300. Following a referendum the same year the two municipalities of Marstal and Ærøskøbing will be merged into one by 2006.

VALDEMARS SLOT

With its great manorial court yard, the huge slate roof, the low buildings around the artificial lake in the centre of the grounds, completed by the beautiful tea pavilion in the lower part of the picture and opposite the main building, the Valdemar castle may appear somewhat overdimensioned in relation to the small, hilly, and romantic Tåsinge island, south of Svendborg, facing the Thurø Sund. However, virtually all the land on the fertile island along with a couple of estates on Funen were once run from here. The castle's predecessor, Kjæstrup, the ramparts of which are located 2 km to the south west, was mentioned for the first time in 1311. The present main building was originally raised in 1635-1643 and built for the favourite son of King Christian IV with Lady Kirsten Munk, Valdemar Christian, after whom the castle is named. Approximately in 1680 the naval hero, Admiral Niels Juel, had the castle renovated. In the 1750's his grandson Niels Iuel transformed the castle into a symmetric construction, including the farm buildings and the tea pavilion. Also, the distinguished interiors and the artificial lake are mainly from this period. The castle has been in the hands of the family Juel/Iuel Brockdorff since 1678. Today it holds a manor museum and some smaller museums of yachting and hunting trophies. The halls can be hired for big parties and spectacles and there is also an excellent restaurant.

ÆRØSKØBING

The old main town of Ærø is the epitome of a Sleeping Beauty, with its well-kept centre of nice, old town houses - the two oldest from 1690 -, and its net-work of narrow copplestone streets and little squares. It is situated almost in the centre of the north coast of the island and on the westside of the bay between the points of Urehoved and Ommels Hoved. From 1522 until its privileges were reduced in 1634, Ærøskøbing had the monopoly on all trade on Ærø. Afterwards, the island was divided, and in reality the town only had access to the part of the island belonging to the Duke of Gottorp. Nevertheless, Ærøskøbing achieved a certain progress through trade with the duchies of Slesvig and Holstein, the Baltic region, and Norway. The effect of the surrender of the Duchies, including the southern parts of Jutland, following the war in 1864, was negative,and today Ærøskøbing with its half-timbered houses, ornamented front doors, and high dormers with their touch of Slesvig architecture, is mainly a tourist town. There are several museums i.a. the Bottle-Ship Collection and the memorial rooms of Hans Billedhugger there is an old post office from 1749, the church with a copper-plated lantern steeple and a Renaissance pulpit from 1634. The town was never big. In 2004 it was the home of only some 1,000 inhabitants, while the municipality counted almost 3,800. Consequently, a referendum in 2003 resulted in a majority in favour of merging Ærøskøbing and Marstal into one municipality.

TRANEKÆR

For nine centuries the old royal castle of Langeland with its Gothic gables and high, oxblood coloured walls has been towering majestically on its mighty castle hill, overlooking the town of Tranekær. The northeast wing (picture, right), with its 3 m thick medieval brick-stone walls, dates back to the first part of the 13th century. From 1232 and for 200 years the castle was a bone of contention between the Danish king and the Southern Jutland dukes descended from King Abel and later the Counts of Holstein. In 1467 Christian I seized the castle by force. From 1672 members of the Ahlefeldt-Laurvig family have been in possession of Tranekær. Buildings were added in the 15th as well as in the 16th centuries, so as to make a four-winged castle. Double moats with palisades and drawbridges and gates surrounded it, making it one of the strongest fortifications in the realm. The gradually delapidating south and east wings were demolished around 1725. The theatre wing was built around 1800. The castle was restored in 1859, when the present tower was built, in 1949 and in the 1970's, when an enormous Middle Age palatine facade was revealed in the southern part of the north wing. There is admittance to the large castle garden outside the moat, and, against a fee, to the art project TICKON, the castle mill, and the castle and souvenir museum called "Souvenariet".

KNUTHENBORG

This manor near Bandholm, on the island of Lolland, south of Zealand, dates back to the 14th century. In 1681 it was acquired by Eggert Christopher von Knuth, one of many German nobles admitted into the service of the Danish absolute king to strengthen his position. 33 years later the family became Counts of Knuthenborg, by then a vast entailed estate. Since then a manor house was built and torn down two times, and today the residence consists of the house depicted on the photograph, which was built in 1872 as a widow's residence. In the park outside the house the present owner has created the country's first safari park with, i.a. zebras, antelopes, rhinoceroses, tigers, elephants, baboons, and many exotic birds - all together an international tourist attraction.

KRENKERUP

The large country estate Krenkerup on the island of Lolland, south of Zealand, originates from a like-named village and was mentioned in 1330. In the village was a manor, the lands of which kept increasing during the ownership of the noble family Gøye, so as to become one of the largest estates in the country, as it is to this day with its approx. 3,500 hectares, half of which is forest. Today the oldest part of the castle from around 1500 constitutes the eastern part of the north wing. About 10 years later, the east wing, the west wing, and the south wing, which later burned down, were added, while the north wing was extended. The beautiful Renaissance stable was built in 1589. In 1631 the north wing was increased by one floor and the octagonal corner tower was added. The whole castle was renovated in 1780. After the Gøye family, the Brahe, Rosenkrantz, Skeel, Reventlow and Hardenberg families in turn have possessed Krenkerup, which was called Hardenberg in the years 1815-1938. The present landowner is R. G. Reventlow-Grinling. There is no admittance to the castle, which is situated in in splendid isolation on its narrow, rectangular bank, surrounded by moats and water.

ÅLHOLM

The assumption, that Ålholm originally was one of King Svend III Grathe's coastal fortresses from the 12th century, has never been confirmed. However, the fortress had probably been there for some time, when the first known sources mention it in 1329. The oldest part of the present High Gothic castle is possibly founded by Count John III the Mild of Holstein, but it was only fully extended by Valdemar IV Atterdag, who took it over in 1347, and by his successors. The east wing with the old castellan's residence is from 1581. Also in the 1580's was the north-eastern tower increased to three floors, while the northwest tower, from the oldest construction, got two floors. Subsequent reconstructions were made in 1779, 1889, and 1943-1944, when the remains of the old south wing, the Margrethe Wing, were renovated. Several dowager queens have had Ålholm at their disposal, as part of their widow pensions. In the years 1726-1996 the castle was in the uninterrupted possession of the Raben-Levetzau family. In the large Ålholm Automobile Museum, established in 1964 in the castle's farm buildings, Stubberupgård, about 250 renovated cars from the 1880's to the post-war times and several old airplanes and salon train waggons are exhibited.

THE GREAT BELT SUSPENSION BRIDGE

The suspension bridge of the Great Belt is the greatest construction of its kind, to date. It constitutes a permanent crossing of the Great Belt, connecting Zealand to the east by the town of Halsskov and Funen to the west by the peninsula of Knudshoved. The construction - from east to west - consists of a 6.5 km long road bridge, the East Bridge, between Halsskov and the island of Sprogø with a main span of 1624 m and two 254 m high tower-like concrete pylons, on this picture reaching up through the clouds. On this stretch the railway traffic passes through the 8 km long eastern tunnel, of which 7.4 km is a drilled tunnel consisting of two parallel tunnel pipes, each one containing a railway track. Sprogø and Funen is connected by the 6.6 km long combined rail and road bridge, the West Bridge. The railway connection through the tunnel and on the West Bridge came in use in 1997 and the suspension bridge one year later. More than 20,000 cars daily pass the Great Belt connection.

Greenhouse Gardening

The size of the island of Masnedø, connected to Falster by the Storstrøm bridge and to Zealand by the Masnedø bridge, is only 1,7 square kilometres. The island is not only able to boast of the big power station Masnedøværket and a windmill park, but also of these large greenhouses.

FARØ BRIDGE

The two Farø bridges, one between Zealand and the until then unnoticed island Farø, the other from Farø to Falster, were inaugurated together in 1985. It is, in other words, not correct to say "the Farø Bridge", since there are two bridges. The one which leads from Zealand east of Vordingborg across the Great Stream, "Storstrømmen", reaches this island of only 93 hectares. The bridge which leaves the small island towards south reaches northern Falster at Ønslev, approximately half way between the old Storstrøm bridge from 1937 and the town of Stubbekøbing. The bridge between Zealand and Farø is 1,596 m long and looks like most other modern Danish bridge constructions. The Farø-Falster bridge, on the picture, however, is a so-called cross-wing bridge with two towers, called pylons, to which a system of wires is attached to keep up the large central section. This central section between the pylons spans no less than 290 m, and the two attached side sections each span 120 m. Furthermore the bridge consists of 15 more sections, traditionally built on pillars. Below the cross-wing bridge there is a maritime passage with an open width of 260 m and a free height of 26 m. As it happens, the same type of structure was used in the construction of the Øresundsbroen, the bridge to Sweden, completed in 2000. Every day 17,000 cars cross the Farø bridges. The railway traffic, however, still uses the old Storstrøm bridge.

CROP CIRCLES

Whether these figures of a circular shape, observed in a field on the island of Møn, are man-made, like other geometric creations in fields with grain or other crops, or if they have another, more uncertain origin, remains to be seen. However, would not humans be involved, somehow? Since approx. 1980, this phenomenon has appeared in several places around the world, mostly in England, and particularly in the area around the pre-historic constructions of Stonehenge, Avebury, and Silbury Hill. In Denmark more than 35 grain-circles have been observed since 1995.

THE CLIFFS OF MØN

The 7-8 km long and 128 m high white cliff along the east coast of the island of Møn, with sheer and occasionally almost vertical flakes of white chalk, with embedded layers of flint, is the Danish equivalent to the white cliffs of Dover in England. The huge formations of white chalk were deposited in the sea during the cretaceous period, about 70 million years ago. The chalk consists of almost pure calcium and mostly is composed of microscopic chalk plates of one celled sea-weed chalk, the so-called crocoites, which lived in the sea during the cretaceous period. Very common are the small colonizing bryozoans, moss animals and fossils of sea urchin, starfish, crinites, and mussels similar to brachiopodas, cuttlefish in the form of thunderstone, also known as belemnites. More rare are remnants of vertebrates. The diversion of the chalk layers is accentuated by flint hillocks, made out of silicon and the silicon mushrooms. During the last Ice Age, the chalk layers were set under pressure, folded and pushed on and above other layers, making the undulating hills of Høje Møn. Ever since, the winds, the weather and the sea have worked on the cliff and washed away the softer layers from the Ice Age. This has contributed to the instability of the cliff with frequent chutes and landslides. All moves on and near the cliff therefore should be made with utmost caution. The cliff and the forest Store Klinteskov, in the hinterland, were acquired by the government in 1980 and now is part of a protected area of 21 square kilometres.

HVIDØRE

Hvidøre is the spacious white villa in the center of the picture, built in 1871. In 1906 it was purchased by the sisters Queen Alaxandra of Great Britain and Empress Mary of Russia, known as Dagmar to the Danes. They were born Princesses of Denmark and wanted a summer residence in their country of birth. After the Bolshevik revolution in Russia Hvidøre became the permanent residence of the Empress. Today it is owned by the big Danish enzyme and insulin manufacturers Novo Nordisk, who use it for conference purposes.

GILLELEJE

Accommodating almost 5,600 inhabitants, the harbour and seaside holiday town Gilleleje is the largest town on the north coast of Zealand, apart from Helsingør, or Elsinore. The town is located on the east side of the northernmost point of Zealand, Gilbjerg Hoved, and is the administrative centre of the Municipality of Græsted–Gilleleje. The original little fisherman's village has experienced a tremendous development since the construction of the fishing harbour in 1873, followed by continuous extensions throughout the 20th century. Gilleleje is the terminal railway station partly for the private owned railways of Gribskovbanen, which has connected Hillerød with Græsted from 1880, and through Kagerup with Gilleleje in 1886, partly for Hornbækbanen, established to run between Helsingør and Hornbæk in 1906 and extended to Gilleleje in 1916. The economic growth of the town is owed to both the regular fishery and the many summer tourists, who are attracted by the magnificent beach. Furthermore, Gilleleje has developed quite a number of fish factories, an engineering industry, a shipyard and a gravel grading operation, apart from hotels, convalescent homes, boarding houses and villas. Gilleleje obtained a place in history because of the many Danish Jews, who were dispatched from here to safety in Sweden in 1943 during the Second World War. The stony shoal, some 2–6 m down, which extends from Gilbjerg Hoved to the northernmost part of the Sound, is called Gilleleje Flak.

TISVILDELEJE

The sea side resort, Tisvildeleje, on the north coast of Zealand at the Kattegat sea, was originally a fishing hamlet, which, nowadays, has grown together with the village Tisvilde, situated 2 km inland to the east. All together 1,800 inhabitants live here permanently, but in the summer the population is increased considerably at this very popular holiday resort. Tisvilde has its name from the old holy spring, Tirs Væld, Spring of the god Tyr, later known as Helene Kilde, Spring of Helen. Tisvildeleje is the end station of the privat railway, Gribskovbanen.

SINGLE-FAMILY HOUSES

Approximately half of the Danish population lives in detached houses and farmhouses, like these in Ålsgårde by the Sound, about 6 km northwest of Helsingør (Elsinore). A little less than one third lives in apartment houses. Of the country's approx. 2.5 million dwellings in 2002, the detached houses represent 41% the apartment houses 39%, terraced, row and semi-detached houses 13%, and farmhouses 5%. The total population of Denmark is 5.4 million.

KRONBORG

Often the legendary Kronborg in Elsinore, known from Hamlet and the hero Ogier the Dane, has been in the searchlight of the media. Likewise in 2000, when the castle was admitted to the World Heritage List of UNESCO, as a building of universal importance in the history of civilization. This former royal castle was built about 1420 under the name Krogen, thus replacing the Flynderborg fortress, just south of Elsinore, dating from the great era of the herring fishery in the Sound during the early Middle Age. The purpose was to secure the northern entrance to the Sound and the collection of the special Sound Toll, introduced in 1429 and abolished as late as 1857, almost 200 years after Denmark's surrender of Skåne (Scania) on the opposite shores, as well as Halland and Blekinge to Sweden. In the years 1574-1585 the castle was thoroughly rebuilt into a four wing Renaissance construction, the strongest fortress and the noblest castle in the Nordic countries. It was partly destroyed by fire in 1629, but was immediately rebuilt and modernised during the reign of King Christian IV. Now it contains the museum Kronborg Slot and the Commerce and Maritime Museum of Kronborg. Up to 2010, it is exposed to a substantial transition into a modern exhibition area. In the basements underneath the castle the sculpture of Ogier the Dane, created by the artist H.P. Pedersen-Dan, is exibited. " Hamlet " has frequently been performed here, both with national and international artists in the leading parts.

FREDENSBORG

Through the times the castle of Fredensborg north of Copenhagen has been the beautiful setting for numerous official events within the royal house of Denmark. Indeed, generation upon generation the castle has been one of the preferred residences of the royal family. By the end of the 19th century Christian IX, "Father-In-Law of Europe", added a particular glamour to the place, as he gathered the European royal houses at the castle. Here he was able to provide the prominent foreign guests with the sensation of Danish hospitality, in a humble but frank atmosphere, in simplicity and directness, far away from secret police and the like. Today, the attention of the public is mainly focused on the castle, when television transmits the official banquets during visits by foreign heads of state, but it is also frequently used as spring and autumn residence by the present royal couple. The oldest parts of the buildings, the central building with the domed hall in the middle and the octagonal square, surrounded by low buildings, was built in 1720-1722 by Frederick IV, in Italian Baroque style. Later in the same century a storey was added to the main building and the court wing, and in 1752 the four corner wings were added. The most recent building is the Orangery from 1995. The public is admitted to the park with its sculptures by Johannes Wiedewelt.

FREDERIKSBORG

Among the numerous castles and manors in the country the beautiful Frederiksborg Castle has a special position. It is built on three little islands in a lake in Hillerød in North Zealand. The castle became even more colourful, when Queen Margrethe in 1996 inaugurated the re-established Baroque garden by the lakeside. Originally this was a manor, Hillerødsholm, which the naval hero, Herluf Trolle, transferred to King Frederik II in exchange for Skovkloster, later named Herlufsholm. The king did not particularly enjoy the late Gothic manor and instead raised a stately castle, of which the buildings on the front islet with the two round towers, the asymmetrical entrance, the tall Tower of Herluf Trolle, the long pantry wing and the garden palace, Badestuen, at the northern entrance, still exist today. The son of Frederik II, Christian IV, actually tore down most of the other buildings and constructed a new castle in Dutch Renaissance in 1602-1625. In 1859 the inside of the main castle burnt down, except the magnificent castle church with the incredibly well preserved Compenius organ from 1610 and the coats-of-arms of the Knights of the Order of the Elephant. It was rebuilt in 1860-1875 and financed by the brewer J.C. Jacobsen, who also financed the installation of the National Museum of History of Frederiksborg, the collection of which with its portraits, historical paintings, inventory and art work, is a mirror of Danish history. The castle belongs to the State, while the Carlsberg Foundation is responsible for the museum.

FREDERIKSBORG GARDEN

The beautiful Frederiksborg castle in Hillerød has become even more attractive since the inauguration in 1996 by Queen Margrethe of the magnificent, renovated Baroque garden beyond the lake, in the central axis opposite the castle. The fountains of the cascade construction, now controlled by computer, springs with 200 cubic metre re-circulated water per hour. When the garden was established in 1720-25 two uphill lakes enabled the royal gardener Johan Cornelius Krieger to create the cascades following the central axis down the sloping grounds which were regulated in four levels. However, after 40 years the fine garden was already overgrown. Other more romantic gardens were made, and only a thorough research in archives in Denmark and abroad made it possible to reestablish the old layout in Baroque style. With 65,000 box trees, 164 yew pyramids, 375 lime trees and 5000 hornbeams, besides numerous beds of historic flowers and bulbous plants, this pearl in European gardening culture, certainly competes with Versailles and Peterhof outside Saint Petersburg, as one of the most impressive garden constructions of the continent.

KARLEBO TOWN HALL

From the 1960's to the 1980's the town area of Kokkedal in the municipality of Karlebo, north of Rungsted and Hørsholm, expanded heavily on former farmland by high rise buildings, detached houses and low apartment blocks. The building complex in the centre of the picture shows the town hall of this municipality. Below a part of the Helsingør-Copenhagen highway is visible; like the coastal railway, it plays an important role for commuters from the municipality working in the Greater Copenhagen area.

THE BASTRUP TOWER

The tower, or the tower ruin, is located at the north side of the Bastrup Lake, west of Farum. Dating from the early 12th century, it is the oldest ruin of this type in North Zealand and it is one of the strongest fortified towers from this troubled period of Northern Europe. It probably made part of a chain of smaller fortresses, protecting travellers from the inlet of Roskilde to the Sound. At the same time it has helped to control the access from Northern Zealand to Central Zealand through its position on a high natural bank, at that time a point almost surrounded by water. With the exception of a donation deed issued by King Niels in 1130 mentioning Ebbo de Bastetorp, of the mighty Hvide family, sources remain silent about the round travertine tower. Some traces of a moat and of frail wooden buildings have been found, however. There are information signs and a parking area next to the ruin.

DYREHAVSBAKKEN

Every summer an estimated 2.5 million people visit the popular amusement park, Dyrehavsbakken, or colloqually, "Bakken", in the park Jægersborg Dyrehave north of Copenhagen. Possibly it began as a market place around the holy spring, Kirsten Pils Kilde, in 1585 according to tradition. However, it was not until the middle of the 18th century, when the pietist King Christian VI banned the gross entertainment around the springs of Vangede and Vartov, north of Copenhagen, that the midsummer rush to Kirsten Pils Kilde seriously increased, attracting jesters, beer tents and various performers. More and more public entertainments were joining, and around 1830 they all moved to the hill east of the spring. The opening of the Tivoli Amusement Park in Copenhagen in 1843 meant a recession for Bakken, and only during the 20th century did the place flourish again, mainly thanks to the arrival of the electric trains to Klampenborg in 1934. The still existing roller coaster was introduced in 1935 and was the most spectacular one in Europe at the time. The same year the satirical theater, Circusrevyen, played for the first time in its tent. The other market tents slowly disappeared and were replaced by shacks and larger establishments. Incidentally the area is limited, due to the protection of Dyrehaven. It is also the consideration for the nearby forest and its animals that decides the season of Bakken which lasts from approx. April 1st to well into August.

EREMITAGEN

Visitors to the park, Jægersborg Dyrehave, north of Copenhagen, as well as the participants, but even more so the curious spectators of the annual sport events, the Hubertus Hunt and the Hermitage Race, have ample opportunity to admire this beautiful hunting cottage from all angles. From all parts of Dyrehaven and from all corners of the surrounding plain the roads lead to the majestically situated house, built in Baroque or rather, early Rococo style. It was built in 1734-1736 by the royal architect Laurids de Thurah, replacing the earlier hunting cottage, built in 1694 for the keen hunter Christian V on the land of the abolished village Stokkerup. The small pond, Stokkerup Kær, southeast of the castle, was originally the village pond, but also the ridged fields of the village may still be noted in the ground of the plain. A special feature was the royal banquet or "Hermitage Device", making the already set tables elevate from the kitchen below, thus allowing the party to dine and rest in the beautifully decorated dining room in privacy - as the French word hermitage indicates - , undisturbed by the serving staff. The Hermitage was frequently used by the royal family and still is today when hunting in Dyrehaven. There is no admittance to the house which today belongs to the state.

LEJRE RESEARCH CENTRE

From May 1st until the end of the October school holidays it is possible to experience ancient Denmark near the beautiful and legendary Lejre in a reconstructed Iron Age village with families living and working in and around the cottages. Several reconstructions and experiments are made around the area to evaluate techniques used in the antiquity and all the time up until the 19th century. The centre was established in 1964 and displays not only the village, but also a sacrificial bog, and various workshops, where craftsmen recreate the tools and clothing of their ancestors. There is a valley, where visitors, adults and children, may hollow log boats and test them, cut wood, grind meal, and many other things. There is also a viking age market place. Every now and again shooting with longbows is demonstrated, as well as war scenes with iron age clothes and weaponry, or tattooing inspired by the pictorial world of the antiquity. In June the centre is the scene of a Speakers Festival, said to be the largest and most spectacular in Denmark.

THE ROSKILDE FESTIVAL

The yearly summer rock festival at the agricultural show ground outside Roskilde town dates back to 1971 and has attracted thousands of people through a display of both great international names and lesser known artists, expected to become important. When the number of visitors was topping in the mid 1990's, more than 100,000 people came here, but subsequently the organisers have limited the number to around 80,000.

SELSØ

This remote manor, close to the protected migratory bird reserve, Selsø Sø, with its untouched nature, east of Skibby, in the district of Horns Herred, Zealand, was originally a bishop's palace and was mentioned for the first time in 1288. At the Reformation in 1536, Selsø was taken over by the Crown and in 1559 it was acquired by Corfitz Ulfeldt of Krogsbølle. The manor was inherited by his brother, Jacob Ulfelt, who moved it further to the east in 1576 where he built the present manor house. Today's appearance, however, is owed to Christian Ludvig Scheel von Plessen who had the manor transformed into Baroque style in 1728-1734 and erected the gate house to the left in the picture. The last noble inhabitant, Agathe von Plessen, deceased in 1829 and from then on, until 1972, when the main building was leased out and subsequently modernised, it was empty with no modern facilities. The tenants up to 1998, Grethe and Bernhard Linder, transformed the property into a manor museum, where not least the hall with its wall paintings and ceiling paintings of the well known Court painter Hendrik Krock, two unique, huge mirrors and the rich stucco ceiling, captures full attention from the numerous visitors. About 300 meters away, most likely where the predecessor of Selsø was located, the Selsø church is situated, the oldest part of which is a three quarter circular travertine apse, in addition to which, according to foundation traces, a circular nave was planned, but never realised.

WIND TURBINES

Windpower became interesting anew during the oil crisis in 1973-1974, and since then Denmark has created a pioneer image for itself with the development of ever larger and more efficient windmills or turbines for the domestic market and for exports. The wind turbines may be placed by themselves or in the so-called turbine parks which may also be situated in shallow parts of the sea, like the marine turbine park near Middelgrunden reef outside Copenhagen, as depicted on this picture. In 2003 the largest Danish marine wind turbine park, so far, consisting of 72 wind mills, each up to 100 m high, was raised on the sand reef Rødsand outside Gedser on the south tip of the Falster island, south of Zealand.

MIDDELGRUNDSFORTET

The 70,000 square meter large, artificial island with its front street along the quay was built 1890-1895 at the north end of the approx. 2 km long, 2 km wide and 2-5 m deep limestone reef, Middelgrunden, between Kongedybet and Hollænderdybet, in the waters outside Copenhagen. Following the construction of Flakfortet further out in the Sound and of the southern fortresses Dragørfortet and Kongelundsfortet the main task of Middelgrundsfortet was to defend the northeast front of Copenhagen against naval attacks. The fortress was in use like this until 1962. From 1968-1984 the Royal Danish Air Force used it as a rocket battery in the defence of the Copenhagen airspace. In 2001 it was sold to a private person who has invested in many activities in order to turn the old fortress into a national attraction with a coffee shop, a floating restaurant, and hotel facilities. In the summer months there is a boat connection from here to Nyhavn in the heart of Copenhagen.

SAND SCULPTURES

Most people, who have spent time at the beach, particularly in their childhood, have tried with mixed success to be the architects of easily perishable sand fortresses and castles. Such designs, however, differ notably from the artistic sand sculptures, created by special sand artists, often of a high international standard. Every year several competitions are arranged on the Danish beaches with the participation of domestic and foreign artists. The above sculpture was raised on the beach near the Arken Museum of Modern Art, south of Copenhagen. Ordinary beach sand is not used for the art works; instead, a particularly fine-grained sand is used, mixed with glue to avoid a collapse at the smallest disturbance. Consequently the art works are more resistant to both rain and hard winds.

GJORSLEV

The fertile peninsula of Stevns, south of Copenhagen, is the location of the manor Gjorslev, with its large late medieval rampart surrounded by moats. Though Gjorslev is considered to be the best preserved and the largest medieval castle still existing in Denmark, it has undergone many changes through the centuries, since it was built around 1400 by the capable chancellor of and closest advisor to Queen Margrethe I, the Bishop of Roskilde, Peder Jensen Lodehat.The manor house, with its 25 metre tall central tower, is made of limestone moulders from Stevns Klint, with belts of stone bricks and in the shape of a Latin cross. The north wing was built in 1638 and was reconstructed in 1715, the pyramid roof of the tower is from 1748, while the south wing was added in 1843, when the west wing was renovated. Finally, in 1874, the pillar hall of the west wing was reconstructed, while the whole complex was equipped with large, pointed arch windows in neo-Gothic style. Inside, the central hall with its star-ribbed vault basically remains intact. Having been a bishops estate, and since 1536 a crown estate, Gjorslev subsequently had various owners, until the Tesdorph family took over in 1925. Today, the Gjorslev Estate encompasses 1,668 hectares, shared by the manor of Gjorslev, Søholm, and Søgaard, and an equal area of forest. During the day time there is access to the park from the south.

VALLØ

Covering an area of 4109 hectares including manor estates, farms, cottages, and not least forests, the Vallø Foundation, south of Køge, belongs to the very largest landed estates in Denmark. Vallø is originally mentioned in 1320. The heavy red walls of the castle, two massive towers, and sheltering moats form a conspicious contrast to the low, ochre-yellow buildings from the 18th and 19th centuries on the castle lane and the 15 hectares of adjoining park. The present southern wing, the towers - one round, the other square - the two southernmost bays of the eastern wing (with an additional floor in 1776) and the bridge across the moat, was built in 1580-1586 by Mette Rosenkrantz, the widow of the statesman Peder Oxe. In the early 17th century the castle was further equipped with another storey and the towers with two floors, while the west wing was extended with two more bays in 1651. The northern wing was built in 1721 and the three wing "White Diocese" in 1735-1738 and increased in height in 1765. Vallø burnt down in 1893, but was rebuilt in1904. The old Watchman's House dates from about 1725, the Doctor's House 1789, the old vicarage with the Foundation's office from 1740 and the Castle Inn from the 19th century. In 1737 Queen Sophie Magdalene turned the castle into a convent for ladies of the nobility, and registration of potential convent ladies is still taking place after of a break of some 30 years. The property was protected in 1981. During daytime the public is admitted to the castle yard and the park.

PRÆSTØ

With its charming, winding streets and the almost unspoiled environment of a small town, Præstø is the epitome of a charming Danish town. It is situated south of Copenhagen on a former island turned peninsula in the beginning of the 1800s on the southern shore of the tree-lined bay of Præstø. The town, which today has about 3,600 inhabitants (the municipality has almost 7,500), was originally mentioned in 1321, and was granted its first known town concessions in 1403. In the lower left part of the picture, is the church of Præstø, previously an monastery church from the middle of the 15th century, which replaced an older construction. The huge chapel extentions on the south side were added in 1510-1520. In the church there are among other things a pulpit in late Renaissance style from 1631, a beautiful altar piece made in 1657 by Abel Schröder den Yngre, a wood carver from Næstved, and a font carved in oak, donated in 1621.

FAKSE LIMESTONE QUARRY

Normally, the scars caused in the landscape by human activity, e.g. gravel extraction, are not very ornamental, but somehow there is a special atmosphere about the largest man-made excavation in Denmark, the one square kilometre large, open and starch white lime stone quarry of Fakse. It is located on the Stevns peninsula south of Copenhagen, facing the bay of Fakse, right on the eastside of the town of Fakse, also spelled Faxe. The limestone is extracted in the 1 kilometre long and 0.5 km wide quarry in the Fakse hills, made of coral limestone, from the upper Dania time, during the cretaceous period, about 64 million years ago. Before excavations - mainly for construction of buildings - started in the 12th century, the hill top was at least 50 metres above its present level. The deposits consist of fossils of mainly moss animals – bryozoans – and corals. Both the moss animal and the coral limestone contain many well preserved fossils – apart from the corals and the bryozoans, also those of crabs, cuttlefish, mussels, snails, sea urchins, echinoderms, brachiopodas, sea mushrooms and, furthermore, teeth of sharks and bony fish. In 1862 – 1864, the harbour and loading terminal Faxe Ladeplads was constructed some 5-6 km away from the quarry, and in 1866 a railroad was extended to the harbour. In 1884 the Faxe Lime Quarry Company Ltd. was established on the initiative of the magnate C.F. Tietgen. Today, most of the limestone is used by the agricultural sector, for quicklime and by the paper industry.

VORDINGBORG CASTLE RUINS

In the 1160's considerable construction works were carried out in several places in the country. One of these sites was Vordingborg, where Valdemar I the Great constructed a large royal castle as part of the fortifications raised along the coasts for protection against the Wendish looting, in particular. The castle in Vordingborg became a popular residence for the kings of the Middle Ages, and Valdemar II the Victorious (king 1202-1241) expanded it to become one of the largest castles in the kingdom. It was in here that he presented the best men of the realm with the newly composed "Law of Jutland" shortly before his death in 1241. Probably in 1362 Valdemar IV Atterdag erected the 26 m and five floors high fortress tower, the "Goose Tower" (centre right), today the only fully intact part of the great medieval fortress and also best preserved fortress tower from the Danish Middle Ages. The tower owes its name to the golden goose which King Valdemar mounted on the tower as an insult to the German Hanseatic towns. Its present figure and the spire, however, is from 1871. Gradually, the castle delapidated, and eventually it was demolished in 1665. In consequence of the protection declared in 1834 of the 30,000 square metres of ruins, large parts of the 700 m long ring wall to the south and east have been saved, partially in a restored condition, along with fundaments of the castle and traces of a Romanesque church from the late 1100s.

GAVNØ

Here, amidst small forests and plantations, next to the rushy margins of the Suså river mouth, an embankment connects the island Gavnø with the mainland. The island is the location of one of Denmark's most magnificently furnished and largest manor houses, and its great manor garden. Thousands of blossoming tulips, narcissuses and hyacinths welcome the many visitors every spring, while the flowers of the season, herbaceous beds, the rose-garden and a sea of begonias are attracting in the summertime and in the autumn. The first mention of Gavnø was made in 1205, and in 1402 it was donated by Queen Margrethe the 1st to the Dominicans for "young ladies of rank", presumably as a four-winged monastery dedicated to St. Agnes. During the Reformation in 1536 it was taken over by the Crown, and was subsequently owned by the families Lindenov and Trolle, until the estate by exchange came into the possession of Knud Thott, whose descendants still own it. It became an entailed estate in 1786 and was a barony 1809-1921. At the end of the 16th century Hans Lindenov modernised the north wing and erected the big, solid corner tower. Otherwise the major part of the present, three-winged Rococo castle with its rich interiors is owed to the well-known land and book collector, Otto Thott, who was the owner from 1737-85. Upon payment of an entry fee, there is admittance to a substantial part of the castle with its large collection of paintings, to the monastery church and the park. Furthermore, there is a butterfly park and a fire-fighter museum.

GISSELFELD

The manor house of Gisselfeld, south of Copenhagen, not far from Næstved, ranks among the proudest and best preserved amongst the defensive, baronial castles, which were built by the magnates of the realm in the years following the civil war, the Count's Fight, in 1534-36. They were built according to some fairly uniform, partly defensive principles to prevent a repetition of the vast destructions of the Count's Fight. The manor had a predecessor, which was probably located further to the north-west. The present manor house complex was built by the statesman, Peder Oxe, in the years 1547-75. Later, several reconstructions and renovations have been made, but the large, three-winged Renaissance building still has its loopholes, scalding holes, and blind tracery staircase gables intact. Amongst the later owners were Christian Count Gyldenløve, who, by his will in 1701, turned Gisselfeld into a foundation supporting unmarried noble ladies. It is still officially administered by a member of his posterity, the Danneskiold-Samsøe family. The listed ladies do not live on the manor, but rather receive an annual pension. The public is admitted to the newly restored tropical greenhouse from 1876, where art exhibitions and other arrangements are held. Furthermore, there are guided tours in the park and in the large nature area of Gisselfeld.

LISELUND

This elegant, thatched country cottage of palatial design, situated on the island of Møn, south of Copenhagen, is surrounded by a romantic park with lakes, canals, bending paths, artificial ruins, fragile bridges, bastions, cottages and cabins, and casual plantations. The builder was the envoy Gérard Pierre Antoine de Bosc de la Calmette, who had Liselund built for his beloved wife, Catharina Elizabeth (Lise) Iselin in 1792-95 from designs by the royal architect, Andreas Kirkerup. Later Liselund served as a summer cottage mainly for artists. From 1938 the house and the park has been an independent institution in private ownership (the Rosenkrantz family). Liselund is also called the 'Old House', as opposed to the 'New House', which was built on the hill above the park in 1886-87. From May till end October tours are made in the Old House with interior decorations and furniture partly designed by the royal decorator, J. C. Lillie. Nowadays, the New House is run as a hotel and restaurant.

Bregentved

The castlelike manor, Bregentved, with its stately three-winged manor house, surrounded by large farm buildings, a substantial park, and distinct avenues of trees, is Denmark's largest, individual landed estate today. The estate covers 62 square kilometres. Bregentved has been in the possession of the Moltke family since 1746, and the present owner is eighth generation. First mention of Bregentved was in 1319, and since then it has been through the hands of some of the leading noble families of the country. Yet, most of the present manor house was only built 1886-1891, but it contains a well-preserved collection of furniture and paintings from the 18th century, to which the public is not admitted. There is, however, free admittance to the extensive park with the newly restored cascade complex on Wednesdays, Saturdays, and Sundays, as well as holidays between 9 am and 6 pm, in the winter till sunset. Bregentved is situated south of Copenhagen, near the school town of Haslev.

CATHEDRAL OF ROSKILDE

Since the beginning of the Middle Ages the royal burial church has towered above Roskilde, the old town of the kings, just west of Copenhagen, and it is still an all-dominating construction, visible from far away. The present cathedral is the last of four churches on this very place, initiated by Bishop Absalon in 1170's, but with the western parts completed only around 1300. The two towers were added during the 14th century, while the steeples were mounted by King Christian IV in 1635-36. Of the many additions, particularly chapels, the Arch of Absalon connecting the bishop's residence with the gallery of the cathedral, is the oldest (from approx. 1210). The church has been the burial church of the Danish royal house since Queen Margrethe I (ruled 1387-1412) and Christian I. As of 1536 (the Reformation) all Danish kings and queens were buried here, with the exception of Caroline Mathilde (died in Celle 1775). Thus, King Frederik IX and Queen Ingrid rest in the royal burial place at the northside of the church. Among the attractions there is reason to mention the choir chairs flanking the sarcophagus of Margrethe, the altar piece in early Renaissance from approx. 1560, the baptismal cast in brass i 1602, and the fine wrought iron gate of Caspar Fincke at the chapel of King Christian IV. Furthermore, here are frescoes from approx. 1250 and up to approx. 1600, as well as the remains of Denmark's oldest organ, from 1555.

LEDREBORG

The present owner of the palatial manor complex of Ledreborg, east of the legendary Lejre on Zealand, is Silvia Munro, who represents the eighth generation of the Holstein family, which acquired the estate in 1740. Since Silvia and her husband John Munro took over the management, Ledreborg has been very much accessible to the public with large outdoor arrangements, summer concerts, and so-called events, such as e.g. the spring fair, "Dwelling And Life Stile". Also, it is possible to make grand dinners, company excursions, and conferences in the elegant interiors and exteriors. In 2003 the foundation Realdania granted 20 million Danish Crowns (2.7 mio. Euro) for the restauration of the terraced garden, which comprises 80 hectares extending down to the Lejre stream. Originally the manor was called Lejregaard, and together with the settlements of Lejre and Udlejre made a small royal fief. In 1741-46 Johan Ludvig Holstein had the manor thoroughly modernised and expanded by the architect J. C. Krieger. The curved pavilion wings, designed by Laurids de Thurah, were added in 1748-50. Ledreborg is situated at the end of Northern Europe's longest linden avenue, 7½ km long. However, only the trees nearest to the castle remain from 1747. The manor house, which was protected in 1973, along with the remaining buildings, the garden, and the adjoining area, had a new roof in 1995.

GARDENS

Close-up photo of gardens at the southern harbour - Sydhavnen - Copenhagen.

TUBORG HARBOUR

For many years there was a permanent ferry link from the harbour in Hellerup to Landskrona on the other side of the Sound, in Sweden. Now the harbour is closed to maritime traffic. The site used to be owned by the highly reputed Tuborg Brewery, now located elsewhere. Instead, a new city district is under construction on the cleared areas of the harbour, with exclusive housing facing the waterfront, office-complexes and a nicely situated primary school. This is a trend, not only characteristic of the Greater Copenhagen harbour areas, but also of other ports around the country, where the old areas no longer serve their original purpose, and gradually are being transformed into rather expensive residential areas and into sites for businesses not associated with maritime activity.

CONTAINERS IN THE PORT OF COPENHAGEN

Like in so many other Danish harbours the Port of Copenhagen harbours almost no traditional commercial vessels. The containers, i.a., have taken over. In 2002 containers represented approximately 5% of Denmark's shipped cargo, most of it loaded or discharged in the ports of Århus, Copenhagen and Aalborg. In the 18 commercial harbours with a total annual turnover of more than one million tonnes, 154,300 containers were discharged, equaling 248,300 TEU (a measurement for the number of containers recalculated into units of 20 ft length) and 155,900 containers were loaded, equaling 250,000 TEU. 60% of the containers had a length of 40 ft. The amount of containerised goods in the Port of Copenhagen was 811,000 tonnes (Århus: 2,162,000 tonnes and Aalborg: 244,000 tonnes). It should be mentioned that Maersk Sealand, owned by the Danish A.P. Møller Group, is the World's biggest container shipping company with approx. 250 container carriers (2002) and considerable logistic operations.

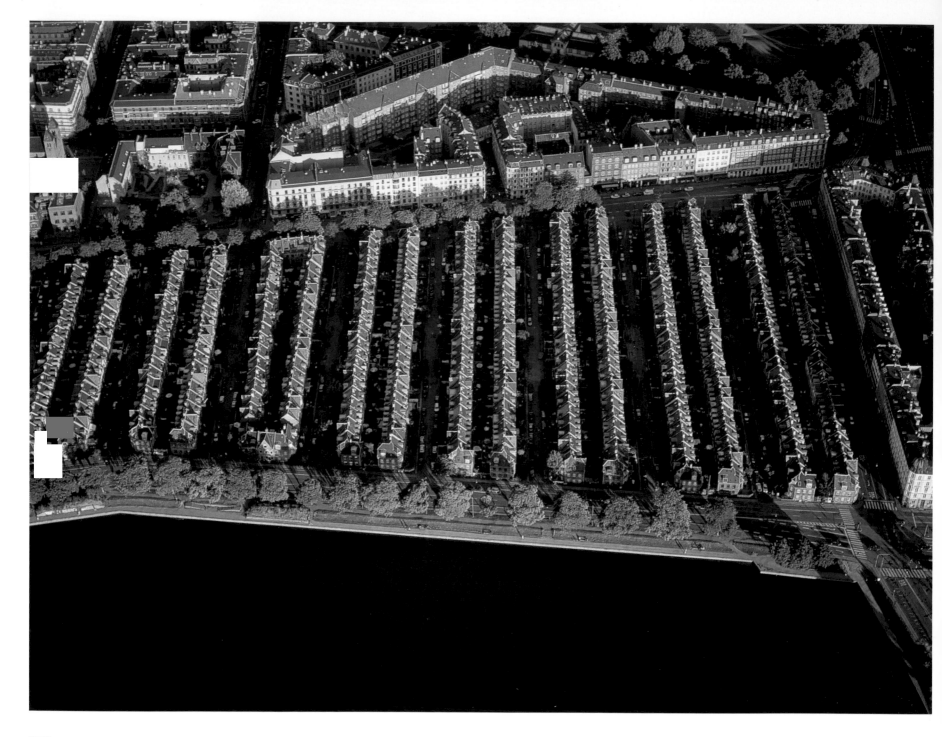

KARTOFFELRÆKKERNE

At the end of the 19th century several quarters with terraced houses were raised with small front gardens and backyards, which seperate each of these identical houses from the one opposite. This was done to counteract the ruthless exploitations of the working class people by the building speculators at that time. Best known are Kartoffelrækkerne or, in English, the Potato Rows: Eleven small, short streets, all named after well known painters, with cosy rows of houses situated between Øster Farimagsgade and Øster Søgade along the Lakes, and stretching from Sølvtorvet to Lille Triangel at Østerbro. The 480 rather identical terraced houses were built in 1873-1889 under the influence of the works of the medical officer, F.F. Ulrik, on the importance and arrangements of the dwelling. He worked at the nearby B&W shipyard. After the Second World War, many new tenants moved in, especially in the 1960's and 1970's, among which many young people living together on a shared basis. In 1974 the houses were offered for sale, and since then most houses have been transformed into single family houses and have become houses much in demand by the middle class. However, several small shops remain in the corner houses facing Øster Farimagsgade, and the inhabitants often meet in the cafés. The name of this quarter is owing to partly the arrangement of the houses in straight, parallel rows, and partly the fact that this former demarcation area had been used for potato growing.

COPENHAGEN OPERAHOUSE

Naturally, it caused quite some attention, when the well-known shipowner Mærsk Mc-Kinney Møller in the late fall of 2000, donated 1,5 billion Danish Crowns (approx. 0.2 billion Euro) to the construction of a new world class opera house. It is located on the centre of Dock Island, next to the former naval base, Holmen, in the port of Copenhagen, facing the royal residence of Amalienborg and the Frederick's Church on the opposite side of the port. The construction started in the autumn of 2001 and is to be completed in October 2004. By then the Opera will be handed over to the Ministry of Culture, and the Royal Theatre will run the operation with the first performance expected to take place in 2005. The total area of the opera house is about 41,000 square meters, spread on 14 floors. There will be more than 100 rooms, including two vast practice halls for opera, two for ballet, one for the Opera Choir and, furthermore, underneath the auditorium a practice hall for the orchestra. Additionally, there will be a large number of smaller practice rooms. The heart of this 38 m high building and its huge "hanging" roof with the prominent 32 m wide eaves above the double bowed, four storied transparent foyer front, will be the main stage and the actual auditorium, accommodating 1,400 spectators. The studio stage will accomodate 200 spectators. The Opera is designed by the world-famous Danish architect Henning Larsen.

TALL SHIP

Copenhagen has a long tradition as a maritime city, even though there no longer are merchantmen landing here. In exchange, many cruise ships do, thus making Langelinie in Copenhagen the most important cruise ship destination in northern Europe today. The photograph, however, shows something entirely different which is one of the participants in a tall ship race with old sailing ships, captured in the water outside the royal residence of Amalienborg to the left.

Amalienborg

This centrally located palace area has been the residence of the royal family ever since the fire of the first Christiansborg castle in 1794. The four identical palaces – a major piece of European Rococo architecture – surround an octagonal square, with the equestrian statue of King Frederick V from 1771, created by the sculpture artist Jacques Saly, in the centre. The palaces are older. They are designed by the architect and royal master builder Nicolai Eigtved and were originally built in 1750-1760, for the noble families, Moltke, Schack, Brockdorff and Levetzau, the names of which are carried by the palaces. Clockwise, from the far left is the palace of Schack (later of Løvenskiold, then of King Christian IX Palace), today the residence of Queen Margrethe and Prince Henrik. Next to it the most distinguished and well-equipped of them all, the Palace of Moltke (Christian VII's Palace), with its royal accommodation for guests and entertainment halls of the royal family; then the Palace of Levetzau (also called Christian VIII's Palace) with the apartments of the Crown Prince Frederick and of Prince Joachim, Her Majesty's Private Library and the museum of the royal family of the Glücksborg line in the period 1863 – 1947. Finally, the Palace of Brockdorff (or Frederick VIII's Palace), where the Crown Prince and his spouse, the Tasmanian born Miss Mary Donaldson, will move in upon renovations. The Frederick or the Marble Church behind, in the centre of the picture, in its present shape was paid by the financial magnate C. F. Tietgen, and inaugurated in 1894.

ROSENBORG

The charming and richly furnished Rosenborg castle in Copenhagen was originally a country cottage built 1606-1607, which Christian IV converted into a castle in Dutch Renaissance style with tall, steepled towers in 1613-34. Today the castle houses the Rosenborg Chronological Collection of the Danish Kings, opened to the public already in 1838, which contains i.a. the Danish royal regalia and the crown jewels, as well as paintings, glassware, china and ivory works from the time of Christian IV until 1863. The section representing the period after 1863 was opened in the wing of Christian VIII at the Amalienborg Palace in 1977.

THE HIRSCHSPRUNG COLLECTION AND THE STATE MUSEUM FOR ART

The smaller building in the lower part of this picture is the art gallery, Den Hirschsprungske Samling, a considerable collection of Danish art from the 19th century with focus on the so-called Golden Age and Skagen painters, which was donated to the Danish government by the tobacco manufacturer Heinrich Hirschsprung and his wife Pauline Hirschsprung in 1902.

The larger building complex in the centre of the picture is the Danish national gallery and main museum of visual art, Statens Museum for Kunst, originating from the Royal Collection of Paintings, which was separated from the Royal Chamber of Art in 1824. After the fire of "The Second" Christiansborg Castle in 1884, the collections were arranged in the building of the architect Vilhelm Dahlerup in the park Østre Anlæg, and was opened to the public in 1896. The museum was reconstructed and extended in 1966-1970, and in 1998 the new modern extension behind the museum was opened - in the lower part of the picture, towards Den Hirschsprungske Samling. The State Museum of Art includes Danish and foreign art from the 14th century and later with works of, among others, Andrea Mantegna, Pieter Bruegel the Elder, Lucas Cranach the Elder, Rubens, Matisse and Emil Nolde. Furthermore, works by prominent Danish artists, as well as the Royal Collection of Prints.

THE BOTANICAL GARDEN, COPENHAGEN

The present University Botanical Garden in Copenhagen is the fourth in the history of the capital. The first one was established in 1600, and in 2000 the present botanical garden from 1872, celebrated its 400-year anniversary by inaugurating a large and modern greenhouse for threatened species of plants and a collection of Thai orchids, donated by the botanist and diplomat Gunnar Seidenfaden. Inside the garden area of 10 hectares, formerly the place of ramparts and fortress moats, is one of Europe's largest collections comprising approx. 22,000 plants of more than 13,000 different species. The old, protected green house with the Palm Tree House (picture, bottom left) was built in 1872-1874 with the greenhouses of John Paxton in London's botanical garden, Kew Gardens, and his enormous Crystal Palace, as models. It was modernised and renovated in 1980-1982. The new green houses in the Botanical Garden of Copenhagen have been built adjacent to the older ones. In Denmark, also the Agricultural University in the municipality of Frederiksberg and the University of Aalborg maintain botanical gardens with collections of living plants for research and teaching, and for diffusion of general knowledge about nature and plants.

Kongens Nytorv

The largest square of Copenhagen was built as a drilling ground of the Copenhagen fortress in 1670. During a reconstruction of the square in 1996-97 in front of the department store Magasin du Nord and the head office of Den Danske Bank, archaeologic research revealed the existence of the oldest fortifications of the city from the early 13th century. The present appearance of the square, with the wooded circle around the equestrian statue of Christian V, king 1670-1699 (in the centre of the picture), is the result of an attempt to recreate an older layout, which was abandoned in 1749. In the meantime, the rather messy square benefited from a helping hand, when an anonymous foundation in 2003 presented a donation of 50 million DKK to finance a badly needed renovation. According to plan the new Kongens Nytorv is to be inaugurated in the summer of 2005. It was in 2002 the first stage of the fully automatic Copenhagen Metro became operational. It runs from Nørreport under Kongens Nytorv to Christianshavn, and from there in two connections to Lergravsparken and Ørestaden on Amager. In 2003, the metro was extended to Frederiksberg and Vanløse. Among the other monumental buildings around the square, the Royal Theatre, built 1872–1874, the oldest part of which was reconstructed in 1981-1986, is to be mentioned, as well as Charlottenborg, with its main wing built in Baroque style in 1672-1677, now the home of the visual art schools and of the Academy of Fine Arts; finally, almost opposite, on the other side of the Nyhavn Canal and Bredgade, the Palace of Count Thott from 1683-1686, now the French embassy.

KASTELLET

In 1996 the European organisation for the preservation of buildings and monuments, Europa Nostra, characterised the northern part of Copenhagen's old fortification, mainly the citadel, Kastellet, as one of the finest and best preserved fortress complexes of Northern Europe. Just before, Europa Nostra had awarded the newly restored Baroque citadel church a diploma for high architectural value. Eventually, in 2001, the entire fortification was honoured with the medaillon of the organisation. Kastellet was founded in 1662-65 with five bastions and two surrounding moats in accordance with a design by the Dutch officer, Henrik Rüse, as an extension of Saint Annae Bastion from the time of Christian IV, some decades earlier. The complex consisted of six batteries, two magazines, Norgesporten - Gate of Norway - and Kongeporten - King's Gate -, through which access still takes place. In 1704 the church was consecrated, and behind it a prison was build, where the overthrown statesman, Johann Friedrich Struensee, i.a., was imprisoned before his execution in 1772. Approx. 1840 more buildings were added, amongst which the still existing Dutch windmill from 1847 on Kongens Bastion, and in 1874 the house of the Main Guard of Copenhagen. However, the old fortress revealed its insufficiency during the English bombardment in 1807, and in 1869 it was decided to close it down as a fortress. Even so, army barracks remained in Kastellet, and today military offices etc are located in this citadel, which is open to the public.

CHRISTIANSBORG

The Christianborg Castle of today, with its tall steepled tower, is situated in the centre of Copenhagen on the "Castle Islet" measuring only 21 hectares. The castle was constructed in neo-Baroque style in 1907-1928. It comprises, i.a., the Danish parliament, "Folketinget", the Supreme Court, and furthermore the reception rooms of the Queen and the Government. There is also the banquet hall with the tapestries by Bjørn Nørgaard, installed in 2000, the Theatre Museum in the former Court Theatre from 1767 and the royal stables and coaches. The castle is located on the place where the original fortress of Absalon was, and later the Castle of Copenhagen. The "First Christiansborg" was built as a four wing Baroque construction in the years 1733-1745; it was the residence castle of the autocratic King Christian VI, but it burnt down in 1794 with the exception of the buildings surrounding the riding grounds. The "Second Christiansborg", three-winged, was built in neo-Classicism in 1805-1828, but it also burned in 1884, only leaving the castle church, which was consecrated in 1826. The church was reopened in 1996 after a fire four years earlier.

RUNDETÅRN

In Købmagergade, across the student hostel Regensen (below left), in the centre of old Copenhagen, the round observatory tower, Rundetårn, is built in conjunction with the Trinity Church. The tower was erected by King Christian IV in 1637-1642 and its architect was possibly the king himself or the architect and sculpturor Hans van Steenwinckel the Younger. Notable is its stepless corkscrew staircase leading to the astronomic observatory on the top of the tower, in use until 1861, and the rebus inscriptions at the top of the wall facing Købmagergade. Translated from Latin, the inscriptions are reading: "Direct, Lord, Wisdom And Justice Into The Heart Of The Crowned King Christian IV". The church, consecrated in 1656, was built for students, with rooms above the nave for the university library. Since 1683 it has functioned as a parish church. Many invaluable instruments and irreplaceable manuscripts were destroyed, when the roof of the church burned during the great fire of the capital in 1728, but the walls remained intact. The Nordic Antiquity Museum, predecessor of the National Museum, was located here in 1807-1832. After a thorough renovation in 1987 the earlier library rooms above the church opened as an exhibition hall. In 1930 the Historical Collection of Astronomy in Rundetårn, documenting the history of Danish astronomy, in particular about Tycho Brahe and Ole Rømer, was opened to the public.

BØRSEN

The green copper roof in the centre of the picture belongs to the 127 m long building of the Stock Exchange, on the "Castle Islet" in the heart of Copenhagen. It was constructed in 1619-1623 by the inveterate builder King Christian IV in Dutch Renaissance, designed by the architect and sculptor brothers, Lorentz and Hans van Steenwinckel the Younger. The famous dragon steeple was added in 1624-1625, while the dormers were not ready before 1640. The Stock Exchange building has been the home of the Danish Chamber of Commerce since 1987. The red building with the copper-roofs, below in the photograph, is a four-storey bank building of the former "Privatbanken", built 1901-1904 with the greatest possible consideration for the stately Renaissance building of the Steenwinkel brothers; it now houses an investment centre of the "Nordea" bank.

CATHEDRAL OF COPENHAGEN

Even though the Cathedral of Copenhagen, also called the Church of Our Lady, is the fifth on this site, it only achieved the dignity of a cathedral in 1924, when the Diocese of Zealand was partitioned. In the early Middle Ages the church was subject to the Cathedral of Roskilde. The first Romanesque church is assumed to have been built in the second part of the 12th century. It burned several times, latest in 1314, upon which a large, Gothic brick church was built, presumably looking much like the Saint Petri Church, Malmö, in Sweden, today. This church lasted until it became the victim of the big fire of Copenhagen in 1728. It was rebuilt in Dutch Baroque and re-consecrated in 1738. A steeple more than 120 meters high, by the architect Laurids de Thurah, was added in 1743-44. However, this church perished, when hit by a fire rocket during the English bombardment in 1807. Using parts of the old walls, the present building was raised in Neo-Classicism by C. F. Hansen. The famous sculptor, Bertel Thorvaldsen, was responsible for the sculptural marble ornamentation with the standing Christ in the apse, the twelve apostles in the sides of the nave, the reliefs in the frontispiece and above the altar. The church - venue of the wedding between Crown Prince Frederick of Denmark and the Tasmanian born Miss Mary Donaldson on May 14th, 2004 - was thoroughly restored in te 1970's.

COPENHAGEN POLICE HEADQUARTERS

The largest police district in Denmark, the Copenhagen Police, resides at Politigården, in this picture slightly to the right of the centre. The building complex, which constitutes a peak in Danish Neoclassicism, was projected by Professor Hack Kampmann and completed in 1924. All over the building there is an effect of contrasts applied with a pronounced artistic sense, the expression of which may appear theatrical to some. As a curiosity, this did inspire the author Hans Scherfig in his novel "The Scorpio" to describe Politigården, which he called "The Yard", as the fortress of the police force.

TYCHO BRAHE PLANETARIUM

Since its opening in 1989 the Tycho Brahe Planetarium has constituted a remarkable profile in the Copenhagen city picture, situated as it is at the southernmost of the city's three lakes, Lake of Saint George, "Sankt Jørgens Sø". It became the second planetarium on Danish soil and the first of its kind. "Stjernekammeret" at Bellahøj school in Copenhagen had already been established in 1937, and in 1993 the the Tycho Brahe Planetarium was followed by the Orion Planetarium in Jels, Southern Jutland, and in 1994 by the planetarium of the Steno Museum in Århus. The planetarium at the lake in Copenhagen is a donation by the will of the former master baker couple Bodil and Helge Pedersen. It comprises ultra-modern and computerized equipment, an Omnimax film-projector, a 23 m wide dome as a film screen above the auditorium, conference rooms, a restaurant, and various exhibition facilities. The architect Knud Munk, who also designed the fountain in the lake outside the planetarium, designed this round building.

CENTRAL COPENHAGEN

- with the Tivoli amusement garden (the green area) in the top centre; top left a corner of the Copenhagen Town Hall, bottom right the SAS Royal Hotel from 1958-60 designed by Arne Jacobsen, and the railway between the Copenhagen Main Station and the Vesterport Station. Tivoli, which annually receives 3.6 mio. guests (2002), was founded in 1843 on part of the old city fortification glacis in front the moat between the districts of Vesterbro and Kalveboderne. The town hall was designed by Martin Nyrop and built in historical or national romantic style in 1892-1905. The first railway in the Kingdom was constructed in 1847 between Roskilde and Copenhagen with the station outside Vesterport. In 1856 the railway was extended to Korsør on Zealand's west coast, and in 1863 northbound tracks from Copenhagen to Lyngby and to Klampenborg were added, both starting at a special station on the north side of today's Vesterbro Passsage. Subsequently, things developed fast, and already in 1864 all stagecoach traffic to and from Copenhagen ceased.

117

ARKEN

Arken, a museum of modern art, is placed near Ishøj, south of Copenhagen, on man-made land in the bay of Køge. With 180,000 visitors (2002) it is one of the most popular museums, only surpassed by Louisiana, Ny Carlsberg Glyptotek and the National Museum of Art. The design of the very untraditional concrete building, drawn by the architect Søren Lund, opened in 1996, resembles a ship on the beach with stern, masts and steel structures. Apart from containing a permanent collection of Danish and foreign art after 1945, the museum arranges special exhibitions and also hosts cultural events and various promotions.

THE BLACK DIAMOND

The architects Schmidt, Hammer & Lassen have designed the National Library of Denmark and the historical book-museum, a striking building adding to the Royal Library (in the centre of the picture) at Slotsholmen, the 'Castle Island', in Copenhagen. It was inaugurated in 1999 and is known as "The Black Diamond" or just "The Diamond", referring to the cover of black polished granite from Zimbabwe on its sloping facade. The Diamond contains not only the library administration, but also reading halls, a concert hall called the Queens Hall, conference rooms, a cafeteria and a bookstore. The National Museum of Photography is located in the basement, while the long wing, "The Fish", stretching along the harbour side, contains institutions like the Danish Folklore Collection, the Danish Society of Language and Literature, and the woman and gender research centre, KVINFO. The old red building behind the Diamond is the main building of the library, built in 1906. The first national library was established by King Frederik III in the 1650's. It was placed in the long parallel building at the upper left, next to Christiansborg, the Government Castle, but later it had to yield to the Royal Archives..

BELLA CENTER

Year after year, since the erection of the first buildings of the Bella Center at Amager Common in 1973-1975, the largest exhibition area in Scandinavia has been ever growing. At the turn of the millenium the floor-space was further expanded from 74,000 sqm to 112,000 flexible sqm. The 17 halls are used for 25-30 yearly fairs and exhibitions especially for industry, service and leisure, and permanent trade fairs or marts, e.g. the two marts for Scandinavian products: the Copenhagen International Fashion Fair and the Scandinavian Furniture Fair. The Center also hosts congresses for up to 6,000 participants in the section Copenhagen Congress Center, built in 2000. The Bella Center, which is the successor of a center building from 1965 in Bellahøj, a little north of the City, has fine parking facilities. So commution to Forum, the exhibition building in Frederiksberg Kommune, is facilitated with the introduction of the Copenhagen Metro in 2002, since visitors may park at the Bella Center at Amager and take the Metro straight to Forum in the city area.

ØRESTADEN

Many people were shaking their heads, when the Law of the Ørestad was passed in in 1992, to develop a new district of Copenhagen on 250 hectares of Amager and Kalvebod Commons, just south of City. The project was instantly initiated by the establishment of the Ørestad Company, owned by the State and the Municipality of Copenhagen. In spite of the short distance to the centre of Copenhagen, sales of the Western Amager land parcels were indeed somewhat slow during the first couple of years. The plots were meant for primarily business and institutional purposes, and for the erection of attractive dwellings of international standard for 20,000 people. However, since the Copenhagen Metro opened in 2002, building activities have increased. A highway and a railway to Zealand and Malmö in Sweden have been constructed, too. The dark building to the left in the picture was raised for the medical company, Ferring, as the first commercial construction out here. In 2002 the erection of Denmark's Radio's new home, DR City, was commenced in the northern part of Ørestaden. This building complex, which spans 124,000 sqm and includes a multi media and a concert house, is expected to be inaugurated in 2006. Also in 2002 the first section of the expansion of the University of Copenhagen was put into service. Plans to move the Royal Archives out here were temporarily given up in 2002. There are, on the other hand, great expectations to the supercentre, Fields, which opens on 115,000 sqm in 2004. In the development plan space has been allocated, furthermore, for a multi-arena with seats for 15,000 spectators.

Copenhagen Town Hall Square

There have always been debates about the design and the arrangements of the capital's town hall square. The presentation to the public of the black buss terminal on the square in the centre of this photo was no exception. The terminal was erected just opposite the main entrance of the town hall, inaugurated in 1905. At that time the Copenhageners were also divided. Some liked it, others not. Today nobody can imagine Copenhagen without its conspicuous town hall.

COPENHAGEN AIRPORT, TERMINAL 3

The Copenhagen airport, its surroundings and connections are continously expanded. Particularly impressive is the new Terminal 3 which connects the transit area with the airport railway station, all of which opened in 1998. Above the giant hall building a 228 m long Delta wing is suspended 28 m above the ground (picture), supported by high steel pillars 22 meters high. From the tip of the wing is direct access to the railway terminal, placed 7.5 meters under the ground with platforms in granite and Italian travertine as wall decoration. In anticipation of the opening of the bridge connecting Denmark to Sweden from the northeast corner of the airport area, the airport was linked to the Danish highway net in 1997.

PLEASURE BOATS

Sailing is one of the favourite occupations of the Danes. Pleasure boats are available in many sizes, but the majority of the Danish yachtsmen own smaller boats like the ones seen here.

Allotment Gardens

Allotment gardens (as in the above picture from Brøndby, west of Copenhagen) is a different kind of small-scale gardening for personal use. These tiny gardens, which all together form a greenbelt, are normally to be found in the outskirts of the major cities. Areas with these allotments are either owned by non-commercial gardening associations or by the municipality or the state, which lets them out for a limited term, typically to tennants in the cities. Originally, the tenants were mostly families from the labour class and craftsmen, who were able to grow their own vegetables here. The first garden allotment association in Denmark was founded in Aalborg in the northern part of Jutland in 1884. Actually, it was the German poor man's gardens from the 1820's for families with many children, which made a model for many allotment gardens in Denmark. Today, most of the greenbelts are located in municipalities with a population exceeding 20,000 inhabitants. Approximately 40,000 such gardens are members of the Allotment Garden Association in Denmark, while a little less are not members.

KØGE

This town at the large bay of Køge, south-west of Copenhagen, is more than the Church of Saint Nicholas from the 13th and 15th centuries and old protected houses. Køge is also an industrial and commercial town, as this photo shows.

THE BRIDGE ACROSS THE SOUND

The inauguration of a permanent link across The Sound, a four lane highway and a double track railway in 2000 resulted in a closer connection between the rest of Scandinavia and Europe and in a direct road connection via the Great Belt bridge from the extreme north to the southernmost Europe without any ferries in between. The construction consists of an artificial peninsula in the Sound east of Copenhagen, a 3.7 km long underwater tunnel, the man-made island of Peberholm, and the depicted 7.8 km long bridge from Peberholm to the south of Sweden at Lernacken. The central part of this two-floor bridge, with the railway below the motorway, is the World's longest cross-braced bridge (picture, with Sweden in the background) for both road and railway traffic, with a main span of 490 m and two 203.5 m high pylons. In 2001 2.7 million vehicles used the bridge. The number is increasing.

HAMMERSHUS

Apart from being the most famous attraction of Bornholm, Hammershus is the largest group of medieval ruins in Denmark. The castle is built on a rocky hill, standing 74 m above sea level and is almost inaccessible from three sides. Only the eastern part offers reasonable access, and therefore the defence system is particularly complex there. Presumably, the oldest sections date back to 1225 and were probably built by the archbishop Anders Sunesen, as a result of crusade policy of King Valdemar the Victorious in the Baltic area. In the Middle Ages, the castle was in the hands of the archbishops and, subsequently, of the kings. In 1522 it was conquered by the counter-king, Christian II. Three years later and until 1576, it was in the possession of the Hansa city of Lübeck. From 1660, the castle was used as a political prison, in 1660-1661 lodging the traitor Corfitz Ulfelt and his spouse, Leonora Christine, daughter of King Christian IV. In 1743, it was decided to tear down the old, run-down and, by then, outdated castle. Thereafter, it served as a quarry, until the ruin in 1822 became protected as a historical monument. The Black Mantel tower belongs to the oldest parts. The castle bridge from the 15th century is the only preserved bridge of its kind, from the Danish middle age. Today, the protected castle area and its nearest surroundings belong to the government. The castle area can be visited all year round and the 750 m long ring wall surrounds an area of 35,000 square metres.

DUEODDE

Bornholm's south-eastern point is famous for its 100 m wide upper beach with dunes up to 15 metres high and its very fine white sand. The light quartz-sand on the several kilometres long and very popular sand beach has been described as "the finest on earth" - the statement may well be true. This sand is so fine and light, that in the past it was used and exported as "writing-sand", that was poured on wet ink on documents, and it was also used in hourglasses. It creaks or "sings", when walked upon. Dueodde is an old dune and sand drift area, stretching 12 km from Snogebæk in the east, to Boderne in the west, where 80 hectares now officially are protected. A distinctive feature of the sand dune areas of Bornholm is the presence of damp hollows between the dune formations, where reed, heather and alder-thicket grow. In the sand drift area many rare plant species grow and thrive between all the summer-cottage areas. In late summer and in autumn many southbound bird migrations pass Odden, small birds as well as birds of prey, while seagulls and wading birds pass by above the Baltic Sea. The present 48.5 m high Dueodde lighthouse, is the tallest of its kind in northern Europe; it was built in 1962. It replaced the Northern Lighthouse, built in 1879, and the additional Southern Lighthouse. The Northern Lighthouse can be visited from April 1 to October 31.

ALLINGE

The twin towns Allinge-Sandvig, located on the northeast coast of Bornholm, initially consisted of two fishing and shipping communities. They were well protected against western winds, by the huge cape of Hammeren and were not far from the Hammershus Castle. They represented an important link to Skåne, southern Sweden. In 1868, the two towns were joined into one municipality, which in 1970 was merged into the municipality of Allinge-Gudhjem. Since January 1, 2003, the entire island of Bornholm has consistituted one big regional municipality. Even if fishing is of declining importance, the fishing industry still plays a considerable role in the economy. The products can be purchased in the characteristic smoking houses of the island. Otherwise the community has placed its faith in the tourist industry, which already began at the end of the 1800's. Since that time, a large number of hotels, boarding houses and holiday cottages have been constructed to the benefit of the many domestic and foreign visitors. Also an open air public swimming pool and a caravan site have emerged. From the harbour there is a ferry connection to Christiansø. The yellow church on the top left of the picture consists of a gothic nave of cut granite, an extension to the west, a tower from the second part of the 16th century, and a transept and a choir from 1892. Half way between Allinge and Sandvig the Madsebakke hill is located with Denmark's largest and most impressive Bronze Age rock carvings. The the hill "Storløkkebakken", around ½ km south of Allinge, as well as Blåholt further inland, also offer rock carvings.

HELLIGDOMSKLIPPERNE

In the summertime, there is a boat connection between Gudhjem and the beautiful area at the 22 m high, vertical Holy Rocks and the spring, Rø Kjijla, to which ill people flocked, particularly in the Middle Ages. Those, who wish to really capture the breathtaking view of the rugged and crumbled rocks, the deep cliffs and the vertical rock pillars, are advised to follow the path along the cliffs in order to admire the 'Elephant's Head', the 6 meter high rock pillar Lyseklippen, the 24 m deep crevice Lyserenden and caves like 'Wet Stove', 'Black Stove' and 'Black Pot'. Further south along the coast, there are several more clefts and bridges next to the Bay of Salene. From the picnic areas tracks lead to the main path along the waterfront. It was a great day for the abundant art life of Bornholm, when Bornholm's Museum of Art in 1993 was able to move into the beautiful and top modern buildings, opposite the Holy Rocks, between Tejn and Gudhjem. Inside the museum, you find many works of famous Bornholm painters, e.g. Michael Ancher, Karl Isakson, Edvard Weie, Oluf Høst, Olaf Rude and Niels Lergaard. However, also contemporary artists and craftsmen are represented.

GUDHJEM

With a little less than 800 inhabitants, the old fishing village of Gudhjem, situated in the strange rocky landscape on the north-east coast of the island of Bornholm, is not a large community. Nonetheless, the population is growing and the number of people visiting the two harbours, with their basins blasted into the rocks, multiplies during the summer months. People flock here to enjoy the idyllic surroundings of colourful and well maintained houses with their characteristic tile roofs, and built on terraces, one above the other. There are steep passages, alleys and the famous fish smoking houses, tempting tourists with freshly smoked herring, such as the dish called " Sun above Gudhjem ". Its mild climate and sheltering rocks, including the 48-metre high Bokul hill above the village, offer good growing conditions for mulberry, fig trees and climbing vines. Gudhjem truly attracts visitors from near and far. First, the fishermen and the traders arrived, then the tourists and the artists. There is indeed much to find here – e.g. the museum of the great painter Oluf Høst (1884 – 1966), opened in 1998, located in his long-standing residence and place of work, the "Nørresand". Further up along the coast, Bornholm's museum of modern art, opposite Helligdomsklipperne, 'The Holy Rocks', certainly calls for a visit. From Gudhjem, there is a boat link to the rocky Ertholmene islands, Christiansø and Frederiksø, some 18 km north-east of Bornholm.

Østerlars Church

The church in Østerlars on the island of Bornholm is the most well know and visited round church. It is also the most distinct defence church and the biggest of all the four round churches on the island. The remaining three churches are Nykirke (Nyker), Nylarskirke (Nylarsker) and Olskirke (Olsker). Outside Bornholm there is one round church on Zealand (Bjernede), one on Funen (Horne) and one in Jutland (Thorsager). A round church is a central church with a circular or a polygon ground plan. This type has been known since ancient times and has been used especially for churches with a particular function, for example christening ceremonies or funerals. The medieval round churches of Bornholm have several floors and also had to serve as storehouses and fortresses. Østerlars church, made of raw granite boulders, with an apse, a round choir and the circular nave, three floors high, was built during the turbulent years towards 1150. The huge roof construction, however, does not date further back than to the 17th century. The later substantially rebuilt porch dates from the end of the middle ages, while the detached bell tower, made of granite boulders with its belfry in half timber, to the right in the picture, is from the 17th century. Since its erection, the church has been shored up further with a large number of buttresses – probably sometime during the 16th and 17th centuries.

GRAVEL GRADING

Measured in volume, the extracted sand, gravel and stone is the largest raw material resources on land in Denmark with an annual production of some 30 million cubic meters. It is followed by the extraction of calcium, chalk, clay, salt and subsoil water. Gravel is defined as a sedimentary type of rock grains of the size of 2 – 64 mm. The degree of rounding of the various types of rock gravel especially depends on the hardness of the grain, on the length of transportation, and on the handling. Gravel deposited in water has round grains, while moraine gravel from water melted during the Ice Age has more defined edges. The crumbled gravel, like that from the Årsdale area on the island of Bornholm, mostly has sharp edges. The processed sand, gravel and stone is mainly used for the cement and concrete products, road and bridge constructions, land filling and port projects. More refined specialty products, such as glass sand, moulding sand and polish are partly made of quartz sand from the centre of Jutland and from Bornholm. In the past Danes extracted brown coal, flint, marl and bog iron ore, too.

CHRISTIANSØ

On top the colourful Kajgade street on Christiansø with the characteristic two-storied yellow limestone barracks, known as Gaden, "The Street", and mainly constructed in the 18th century. On the picture to the right Gaden of Christiansø is seen from further up. The island to the left is Frederiksø, connected to the larger Christiansø island by a swing-bridge. Below, to the left of Frederiksø, is the uninhabited rock of Lilleø, and above this, Vesterskær. On the top left, the somewhat larger rock island of Græsholmen is faintly noticed. Because of the presence of the two alcidae birds, the razorbill and the guillemot, the island has been made a scientific reserve.